Junji Ito Collection

伊藤潤二 *A HORROR COLORING BOOK*

JUNJI ITO COLLECTION
A HORROR COLORING BOOK

ISBN: 9781789099720

Published by Titan Books

A division of Titan Publishing Group Ltd.
144 Southwark St.
London
SE1 0UP

First edition: June 2022

9 8 7 6 5 4 3 2 1

DID YOU ENJOY THIS BOOK?

We love to hear from our readers. Please e-mail us at: readerfeedback@titanemail.
com or write to Reader Feedback at the above address.

To receive advance information, news, competitions, and exclusive offers online,
please sign up for the Titan newsletter on our website: www.titanbooks.com

A CIP catalogue record for this title is available from the British Library.

Printed and bound in the UK.

Junji Ito Collection

伊藤潤二 A HORROR COLORING BOOK

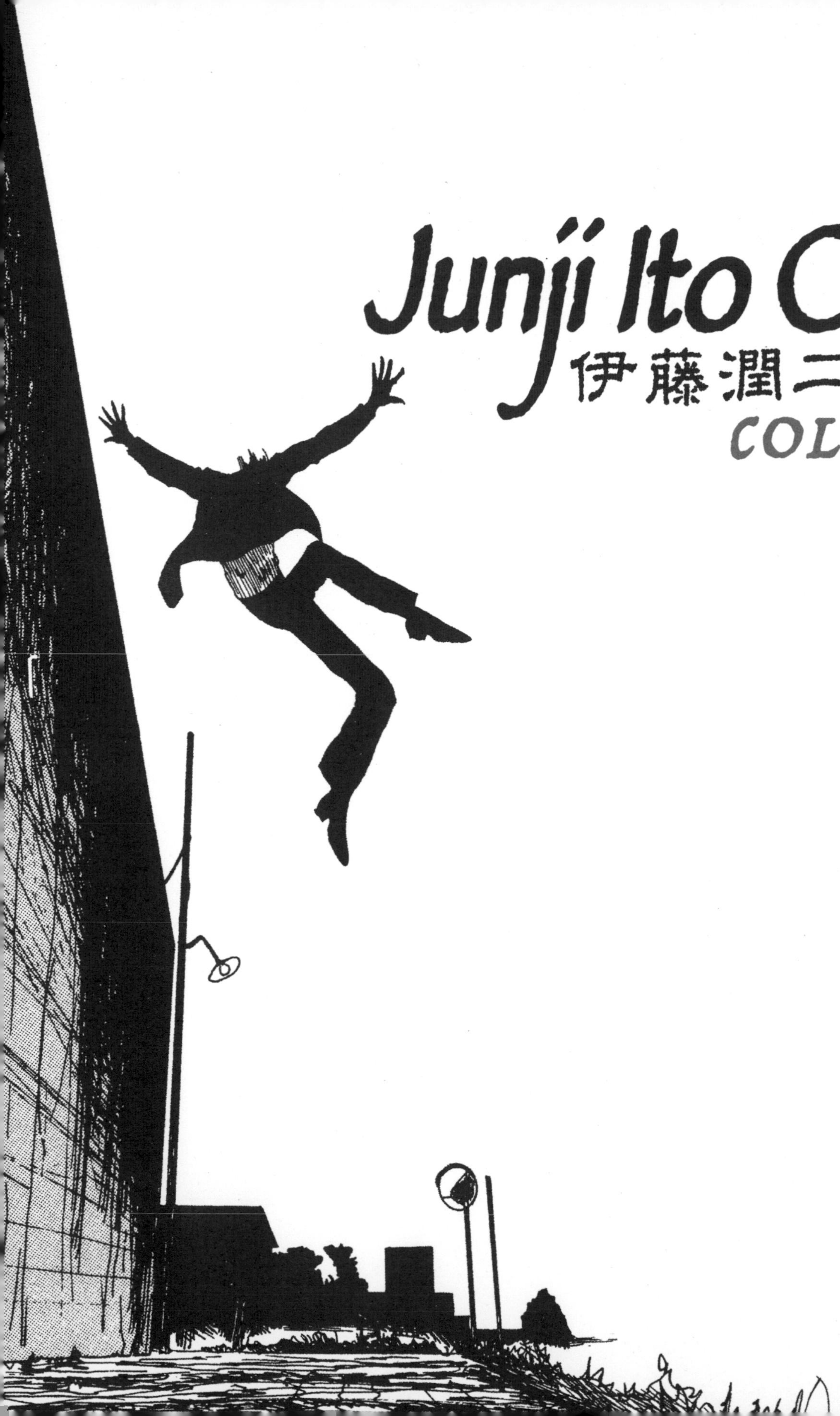

TITAN BOOKS

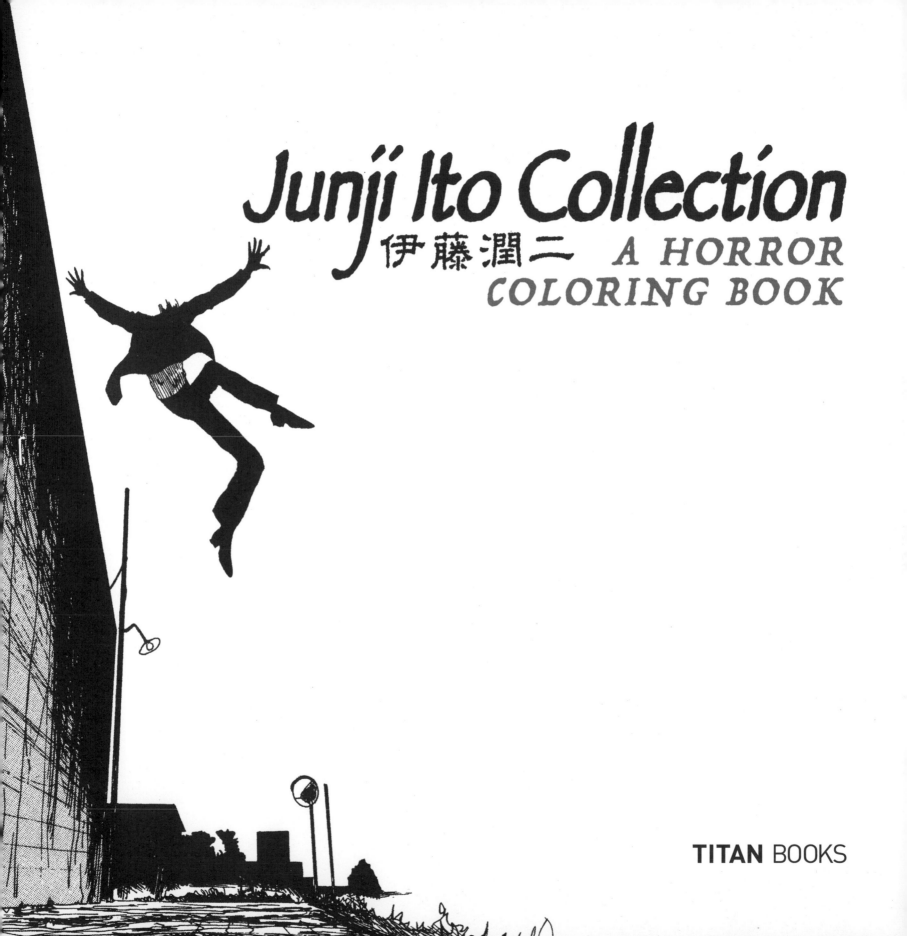

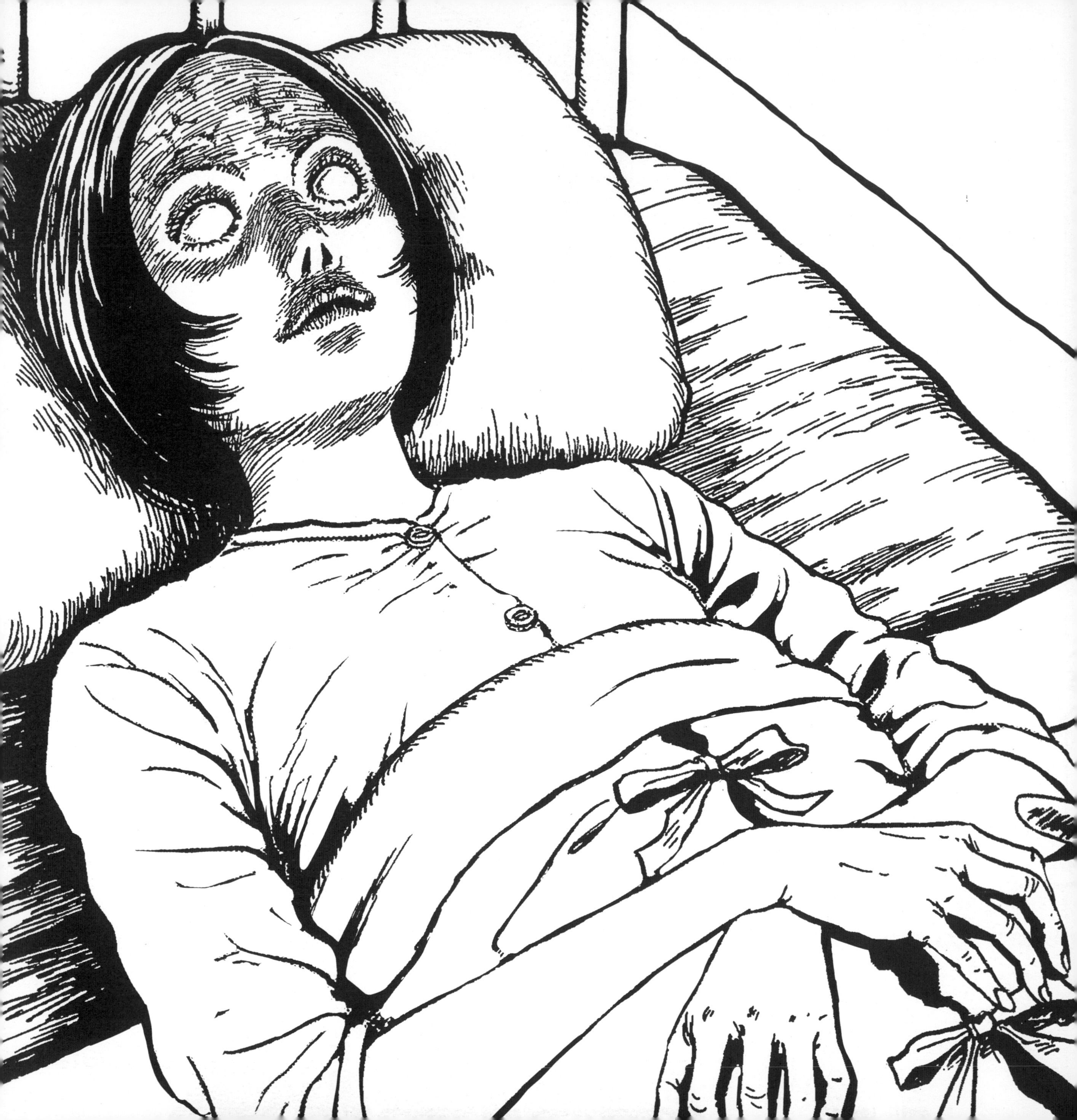

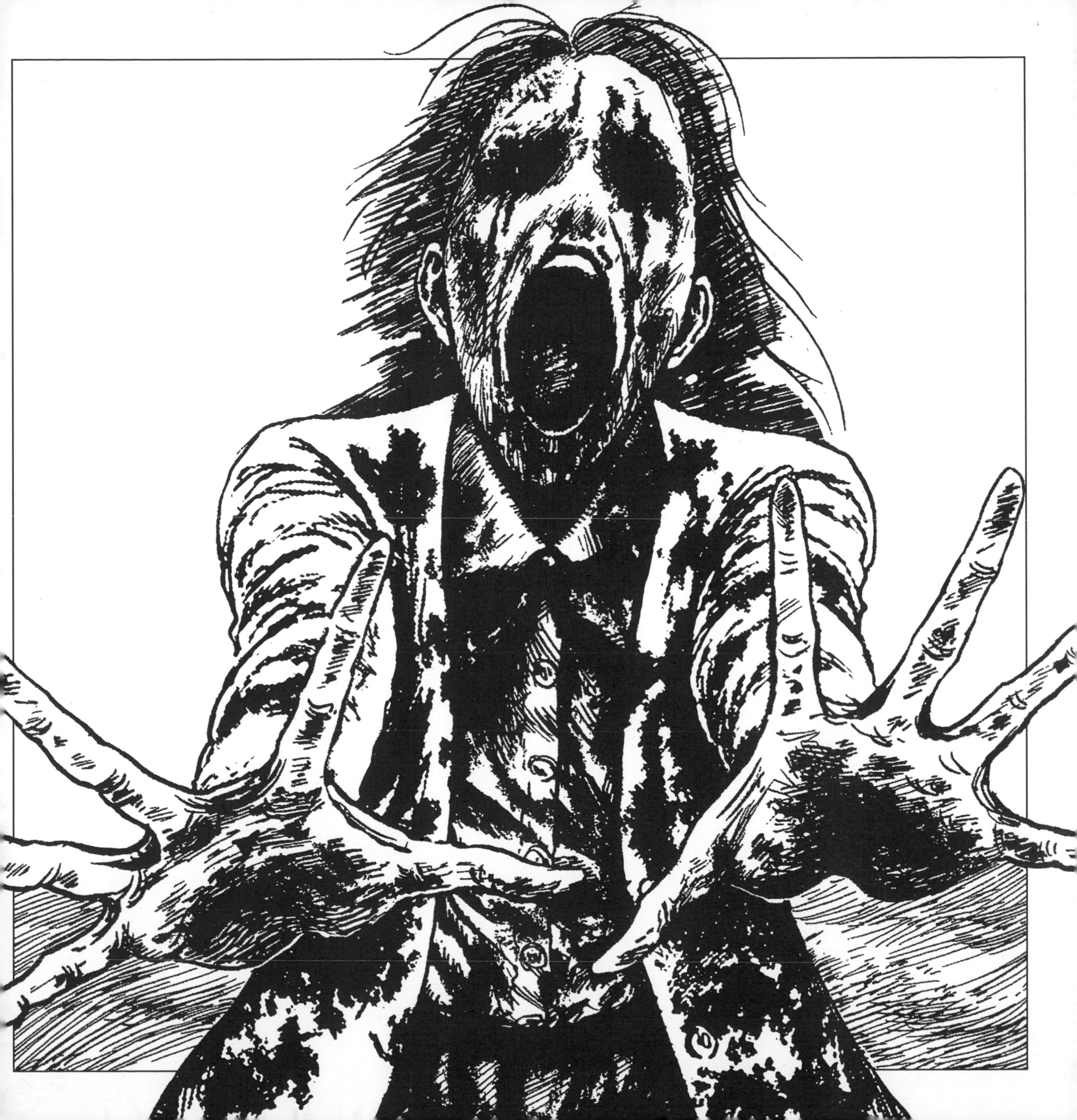

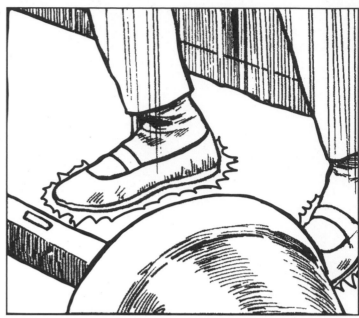

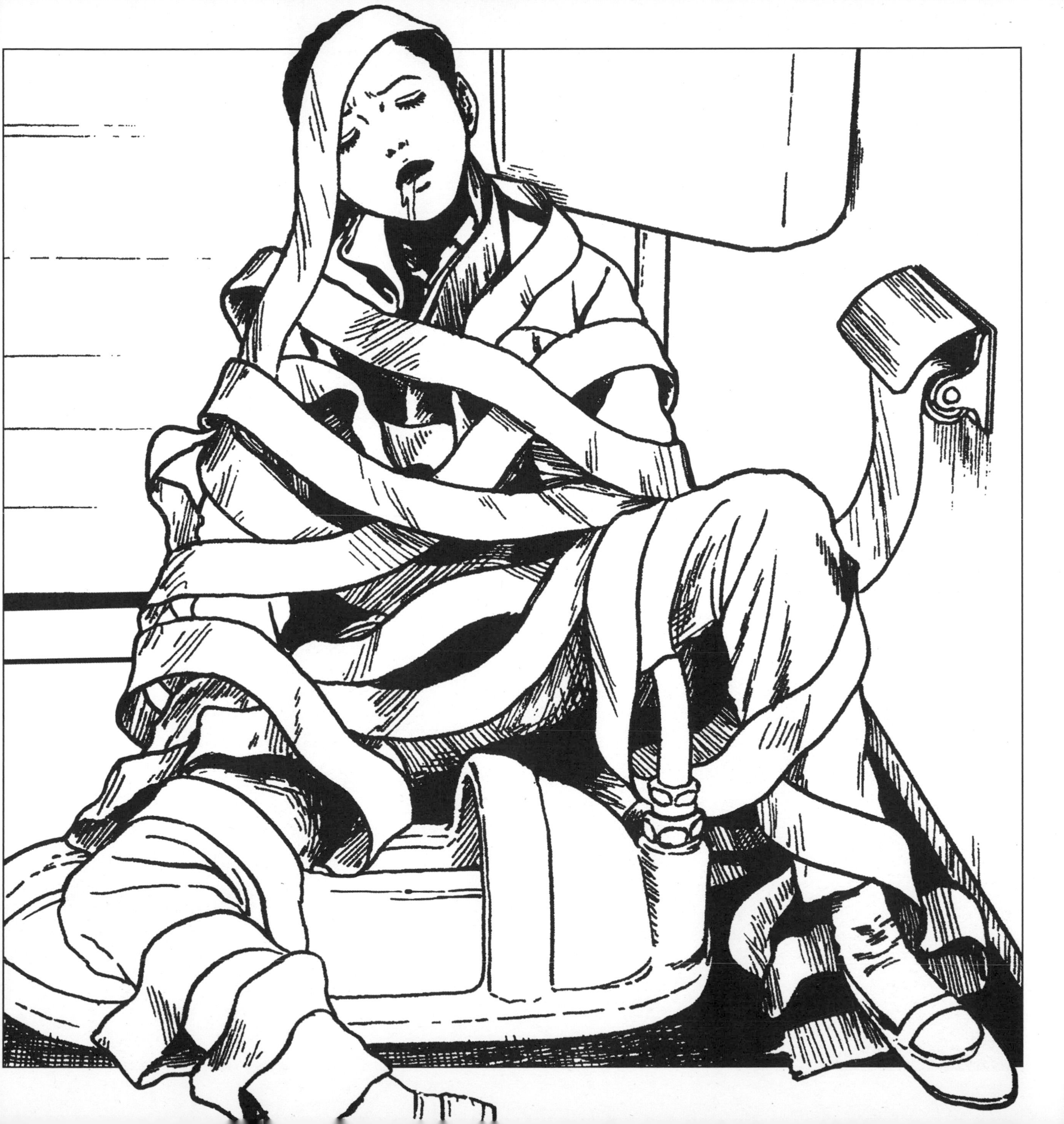

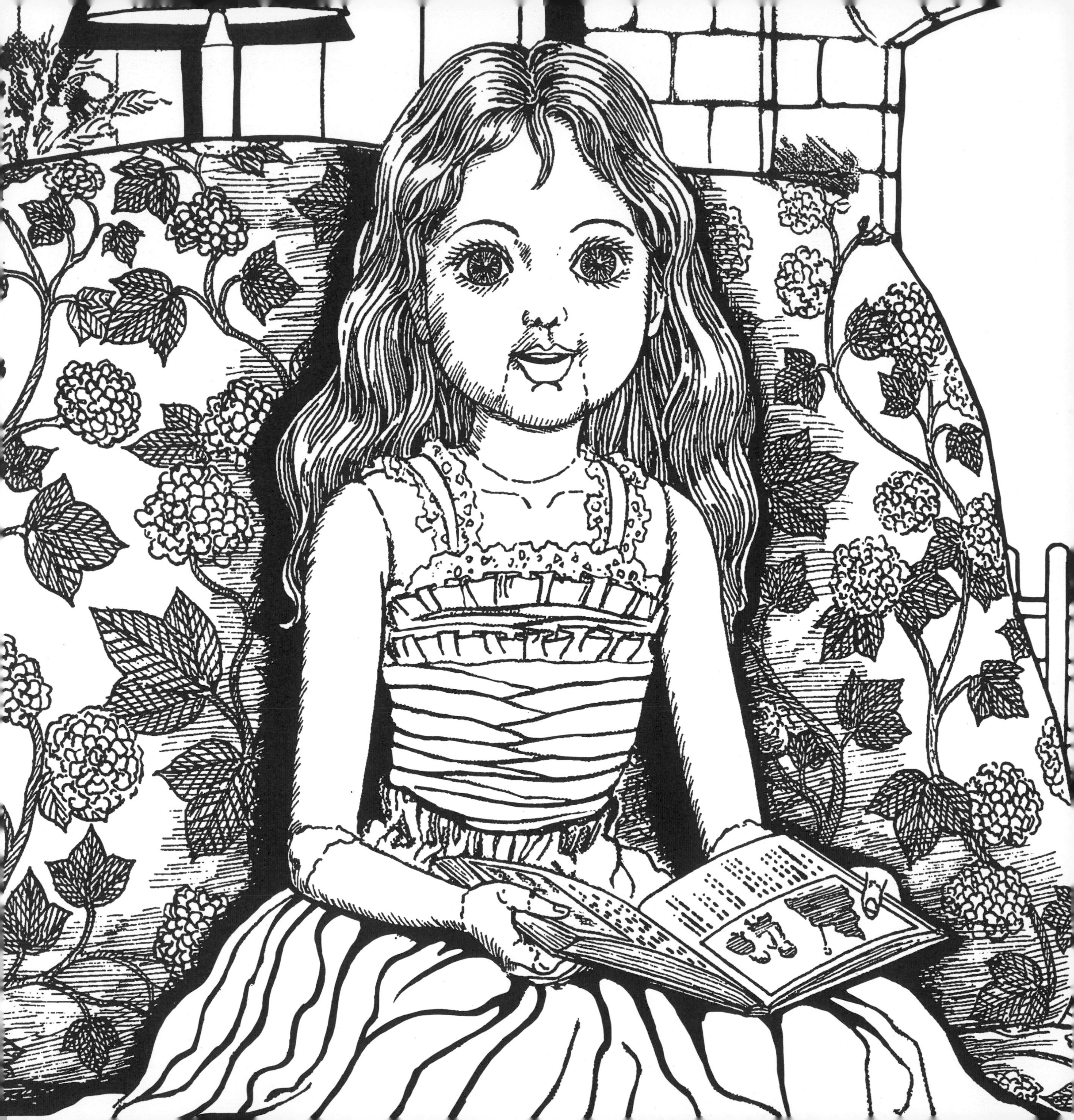

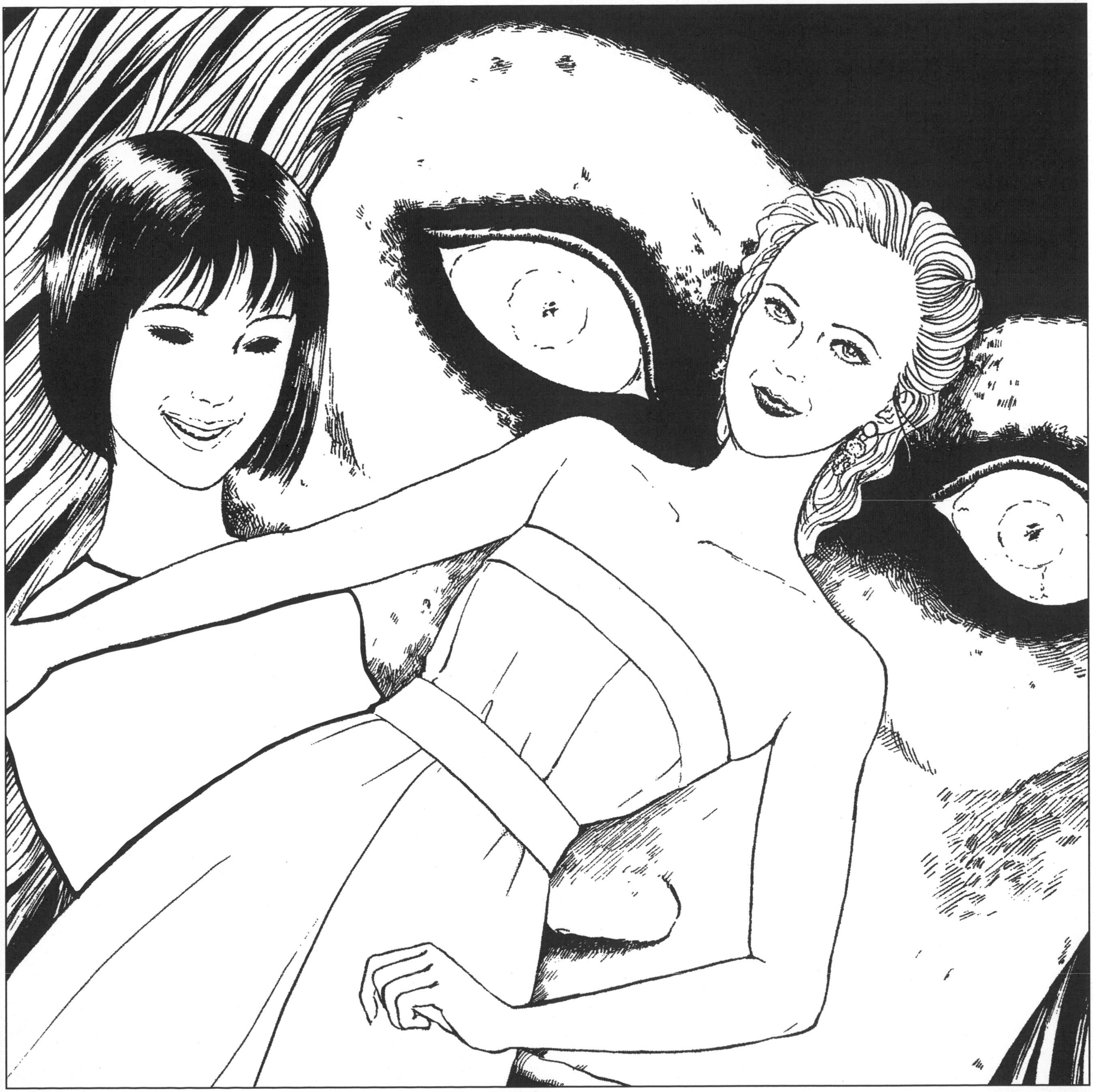

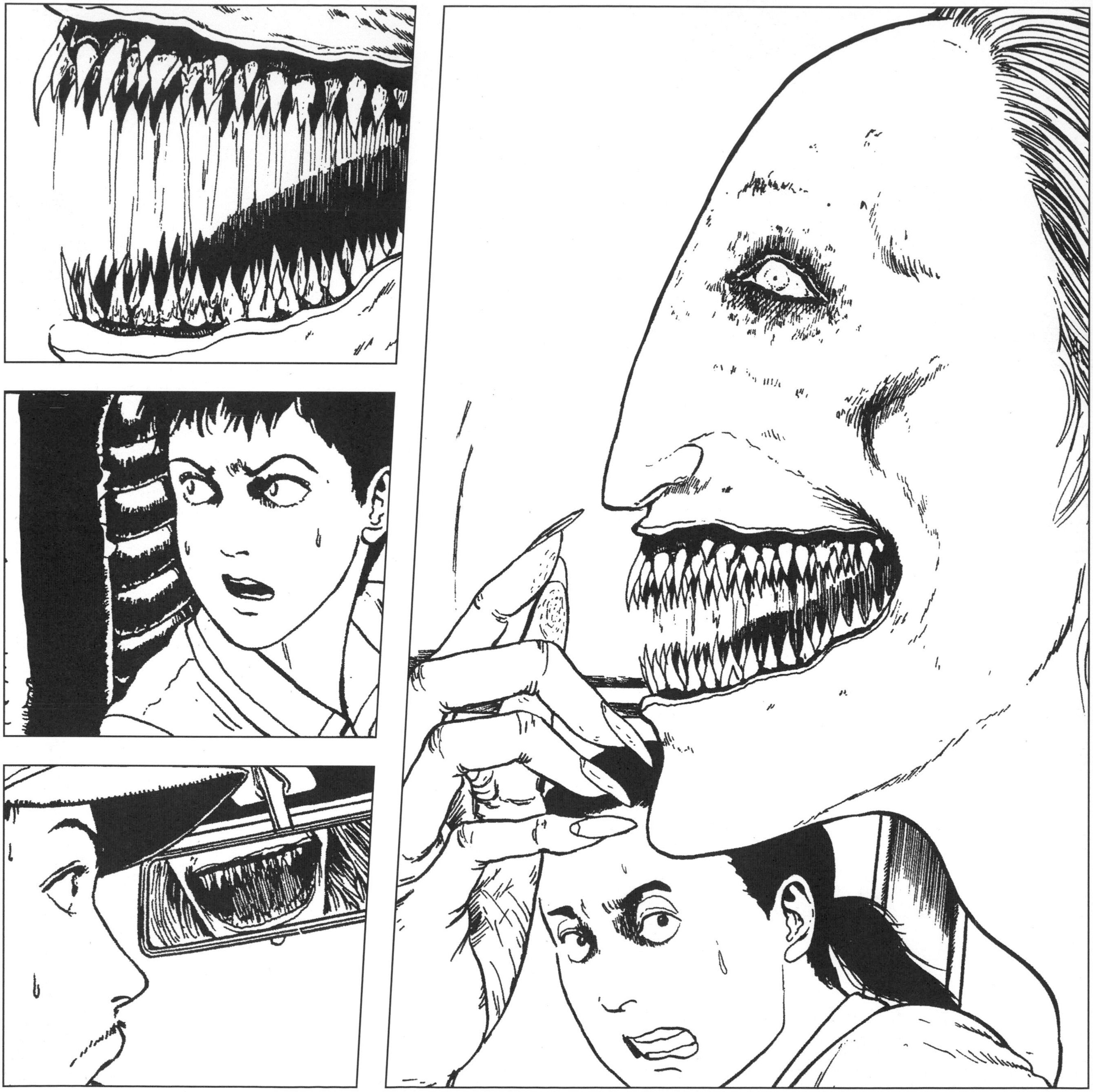

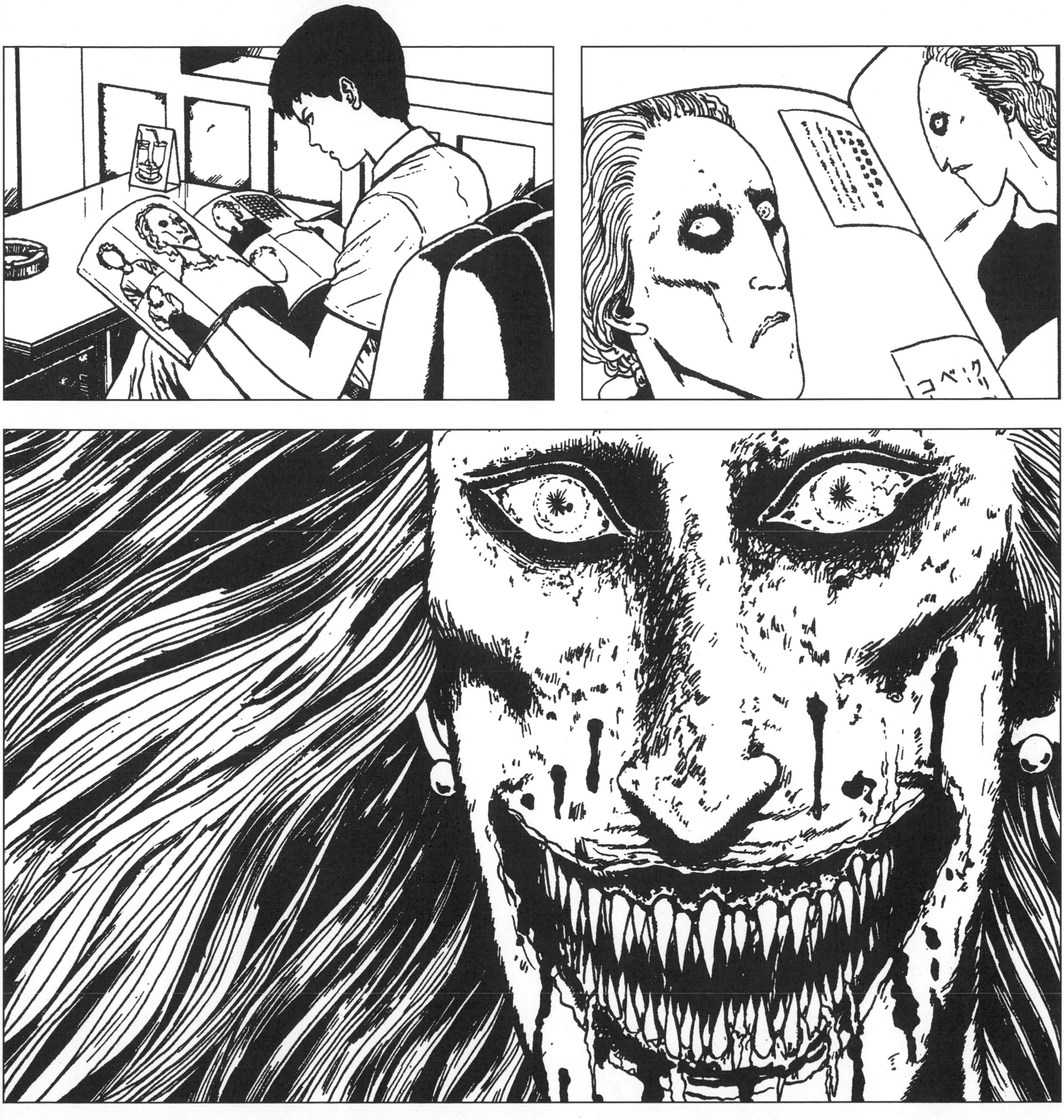

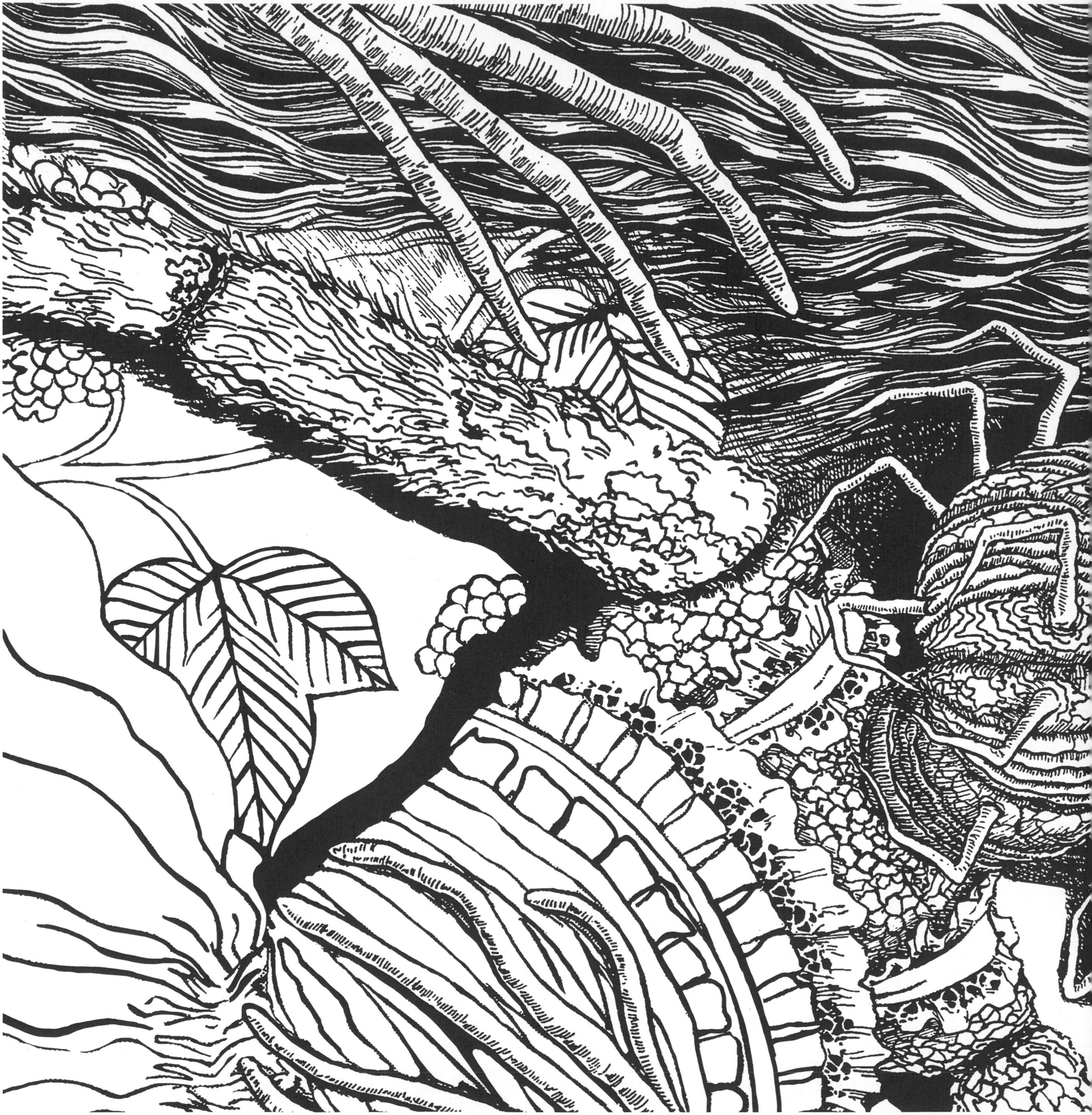

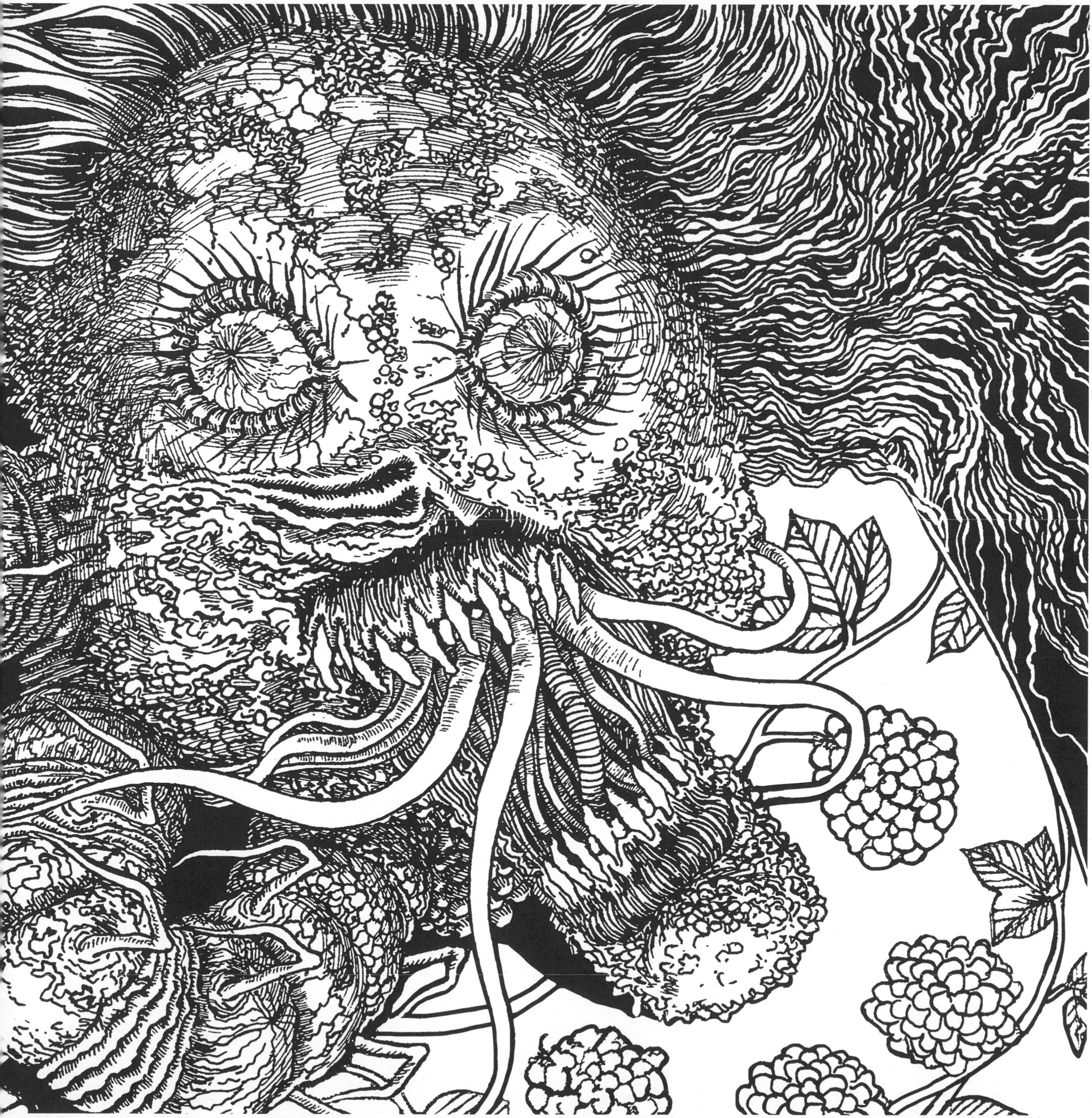

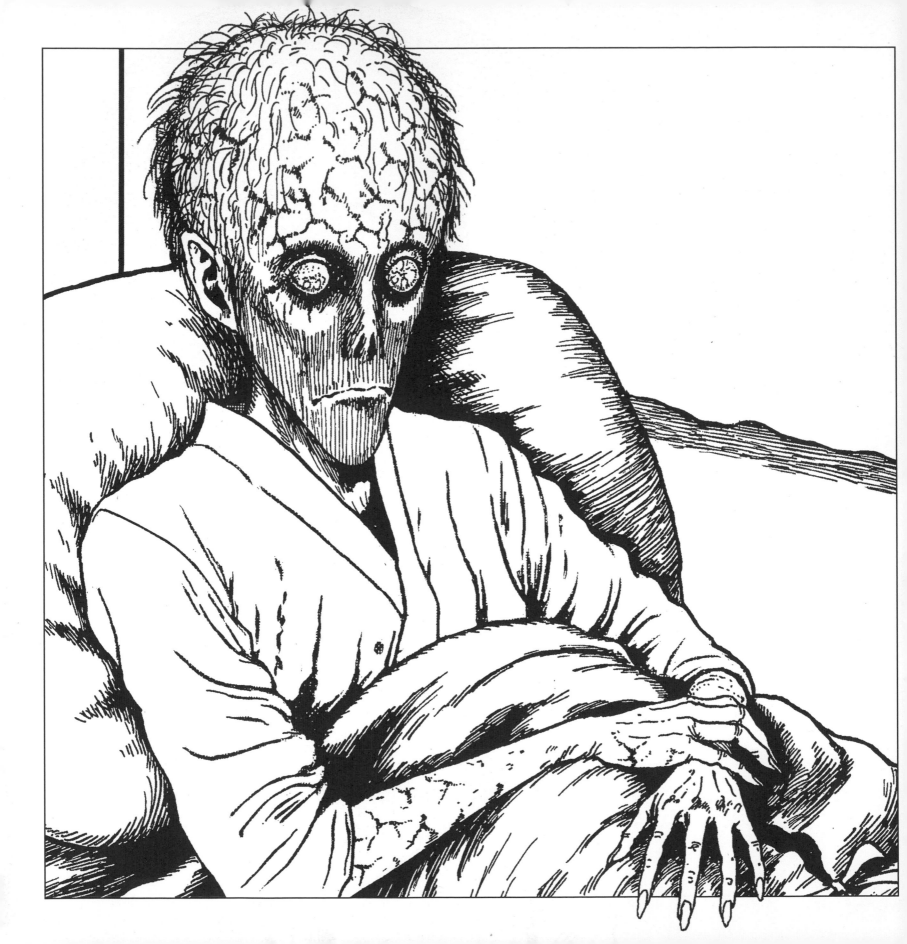

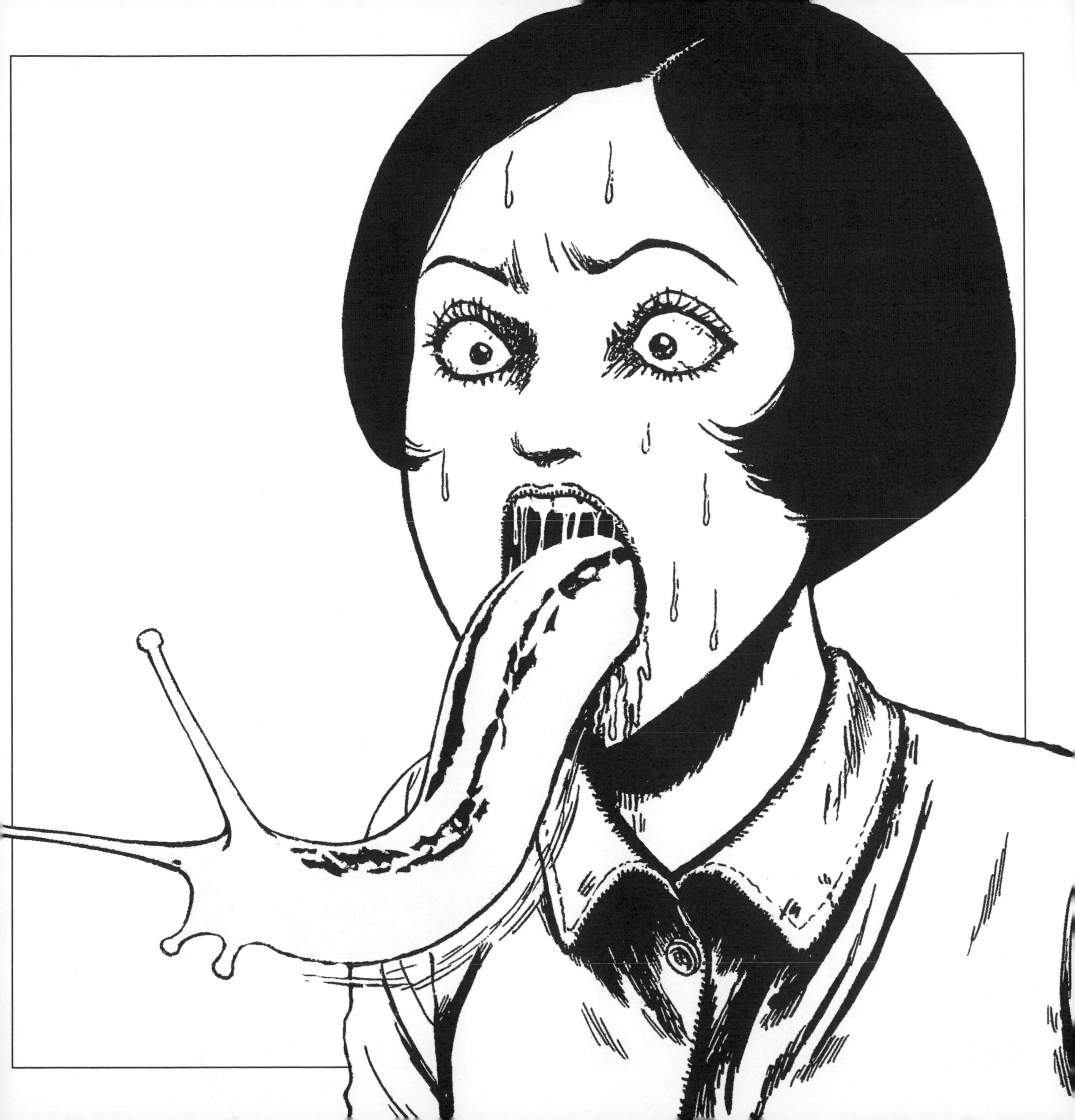

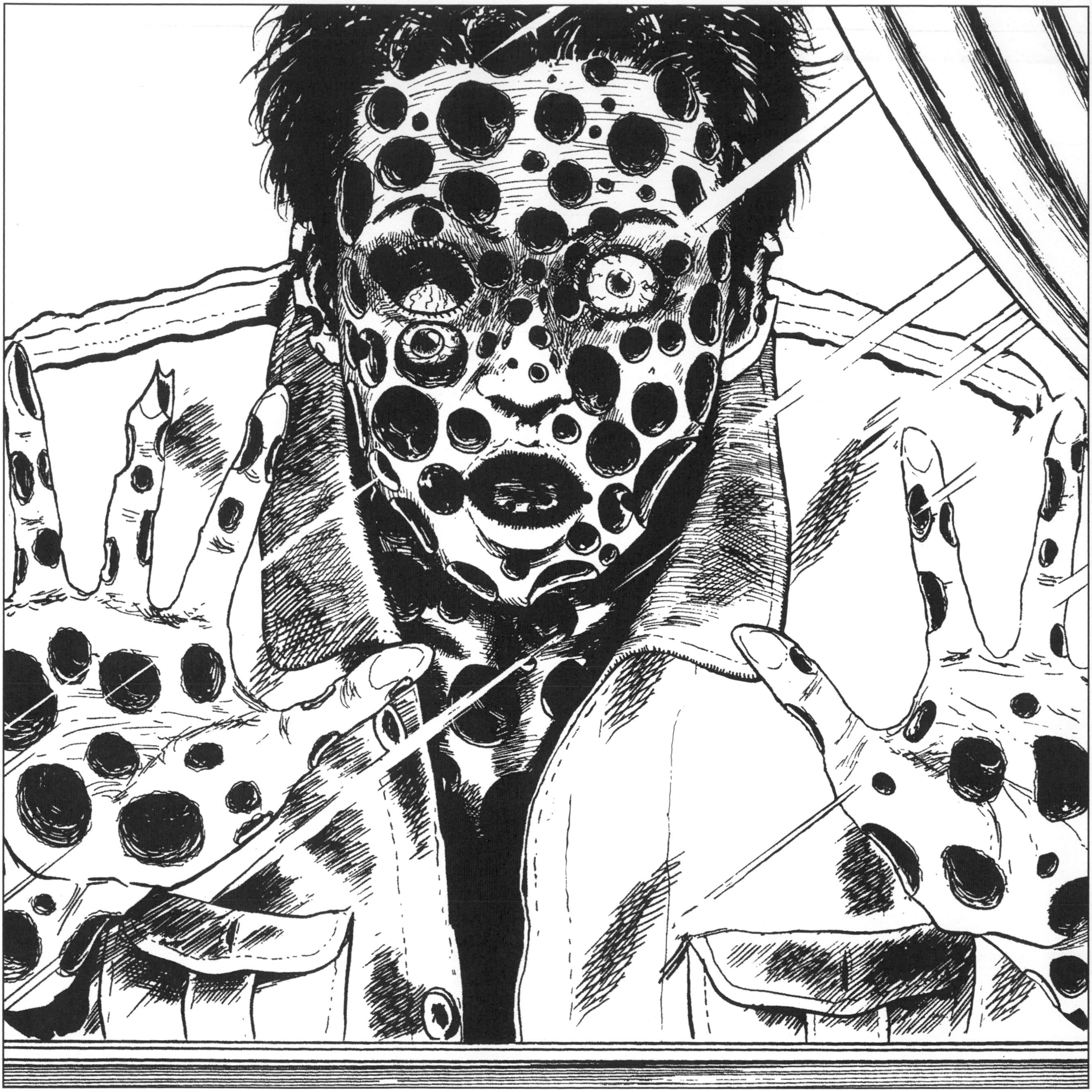

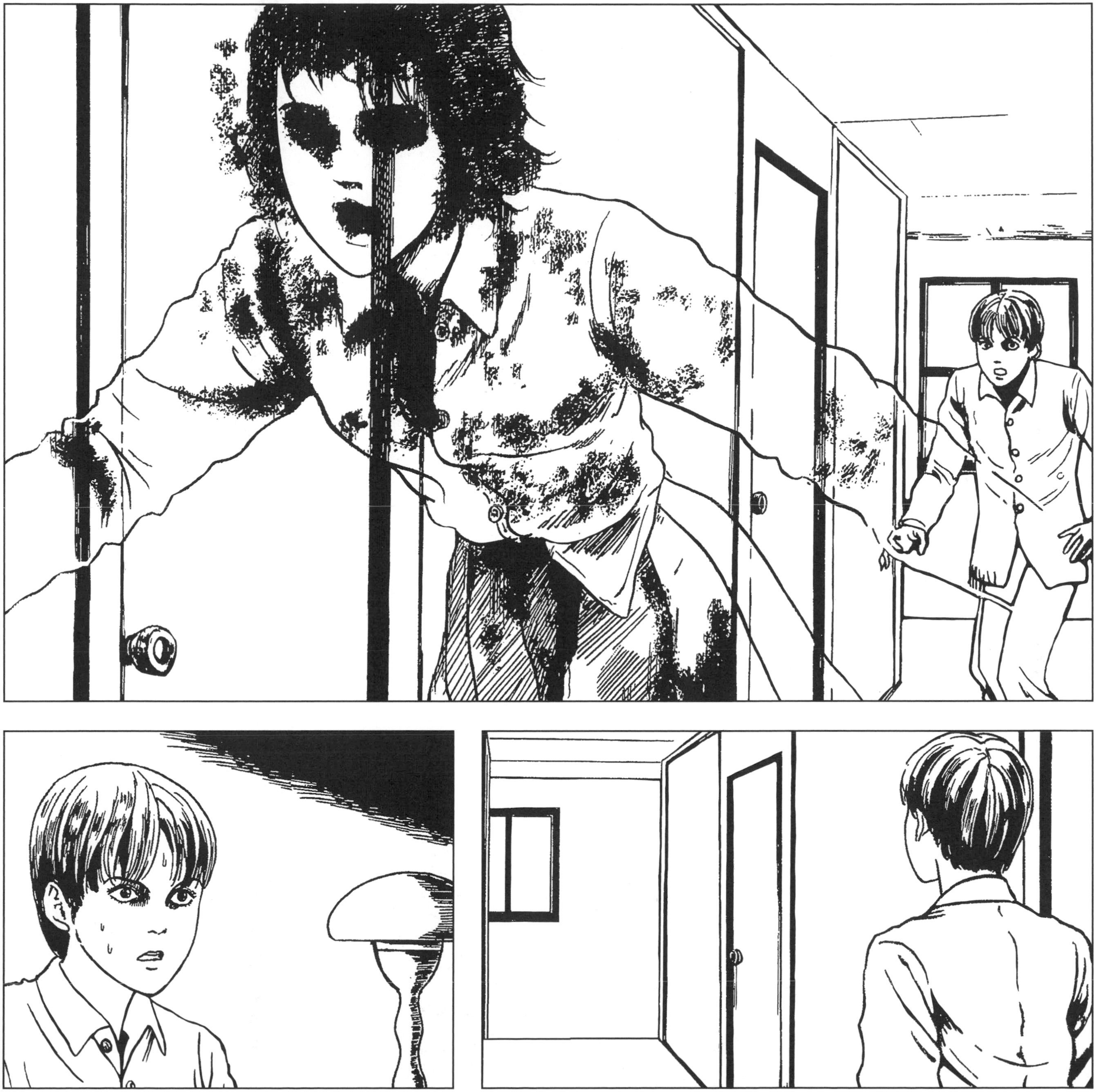

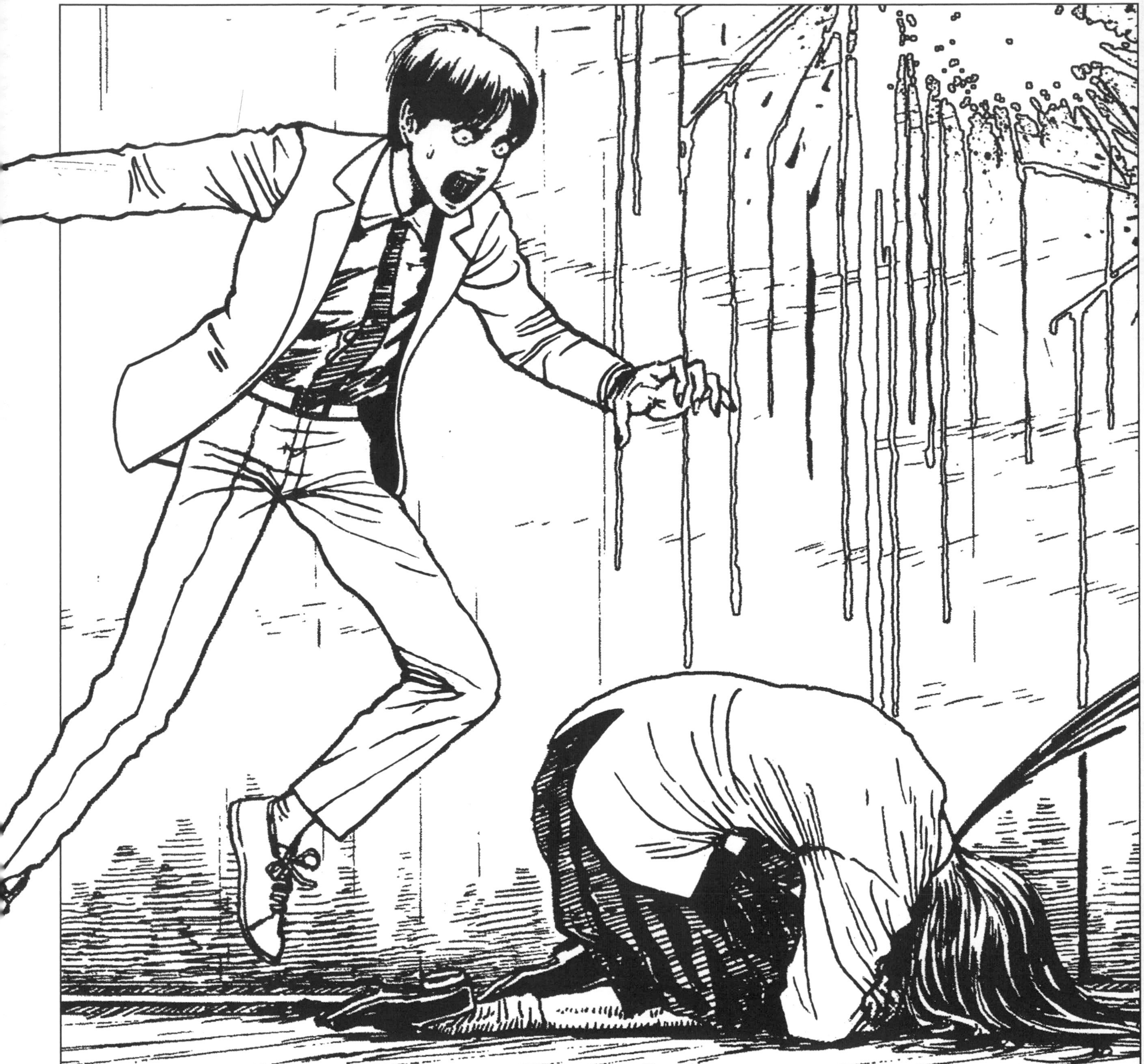

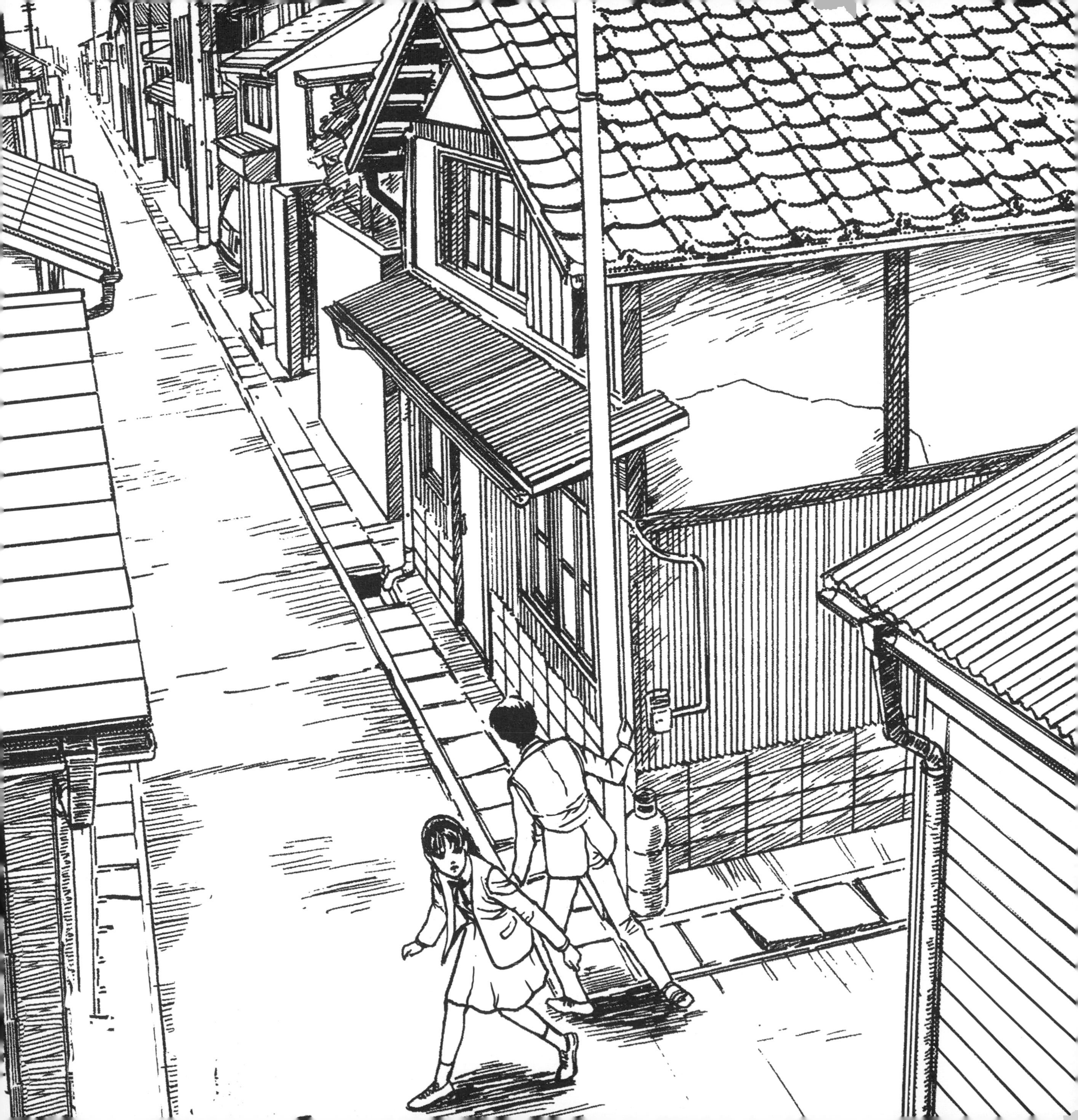

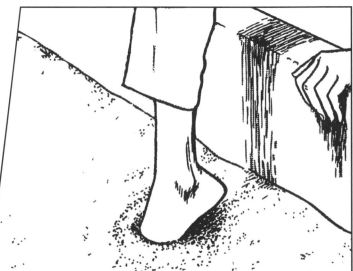

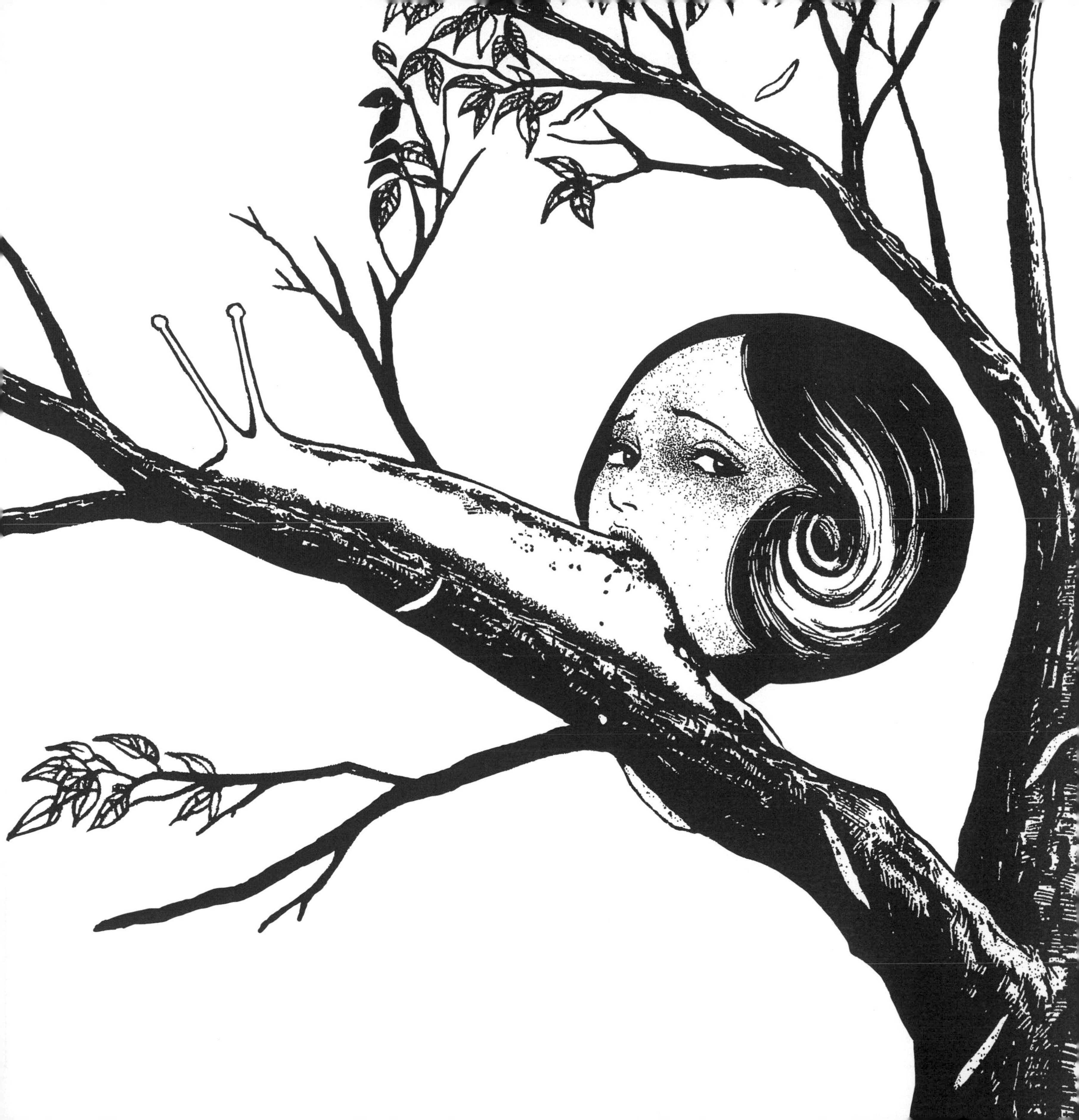

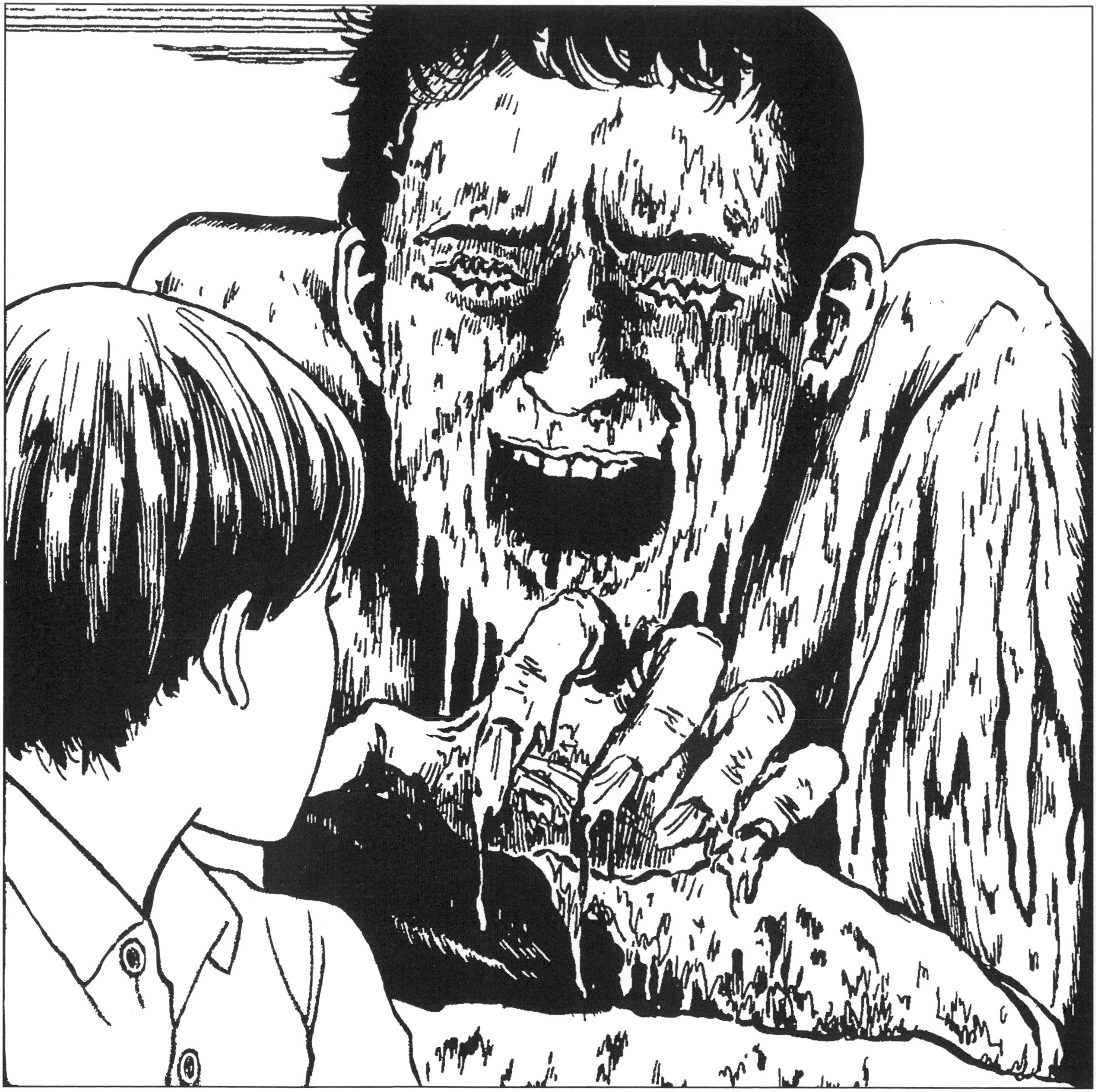

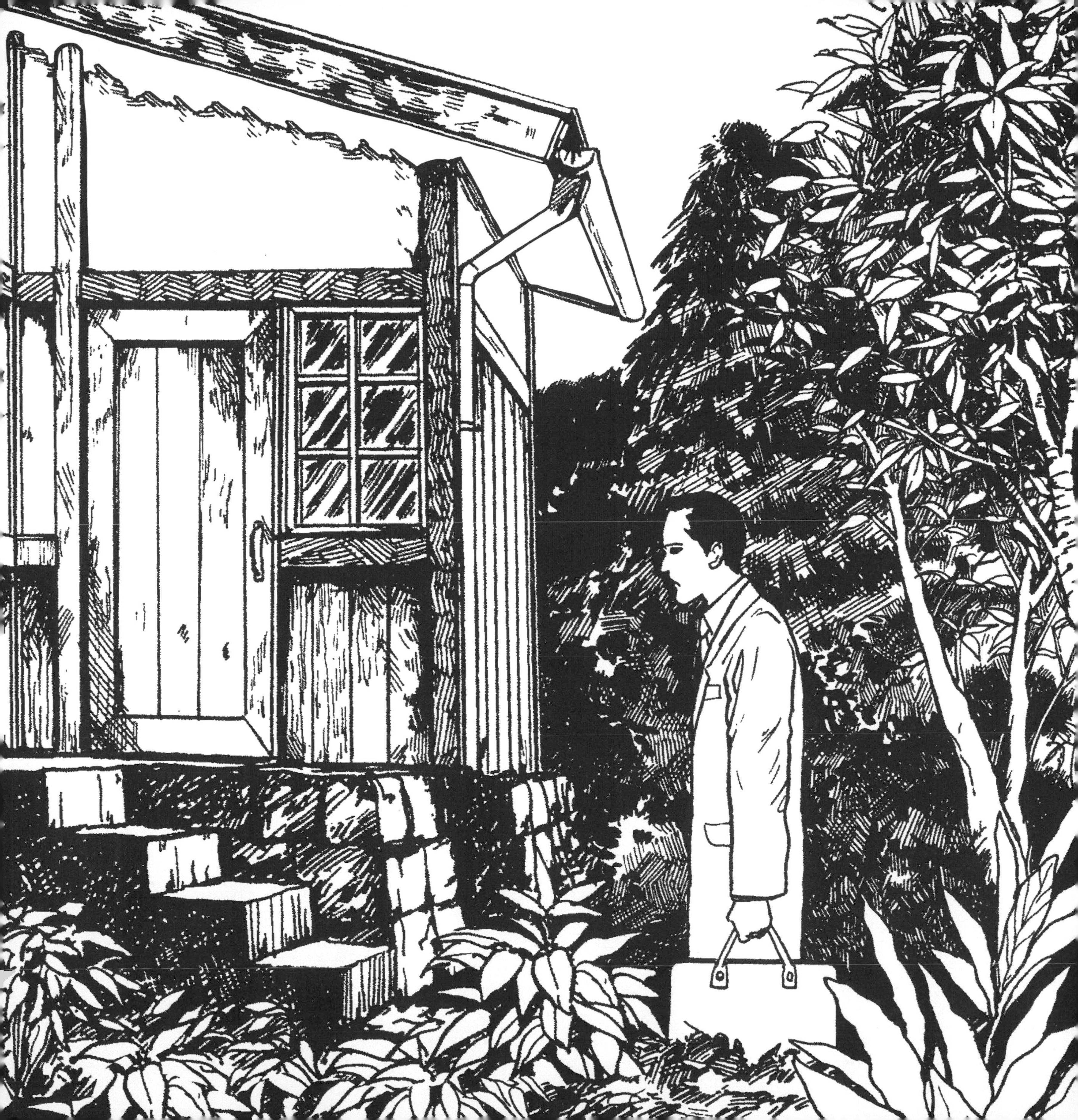

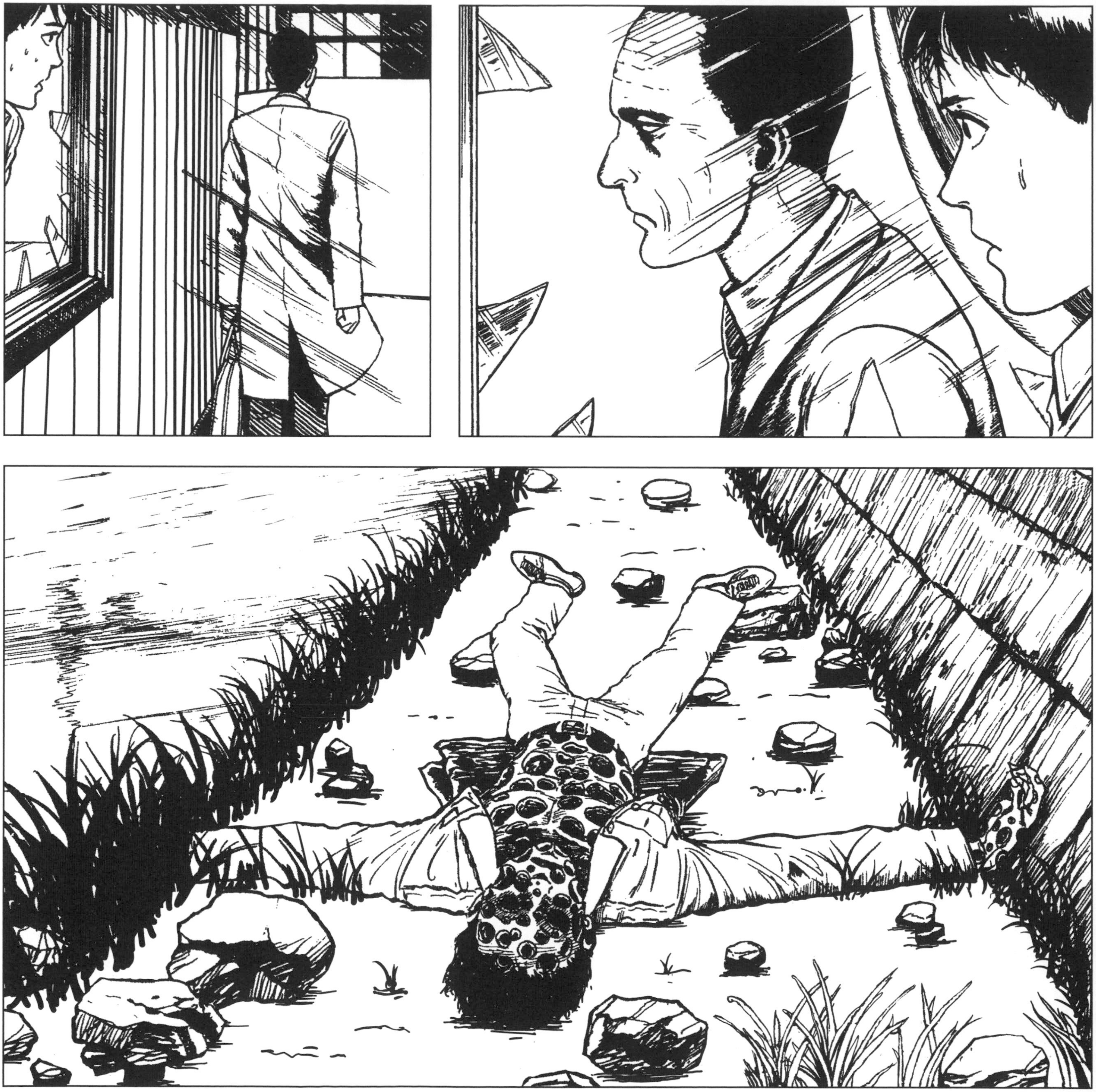

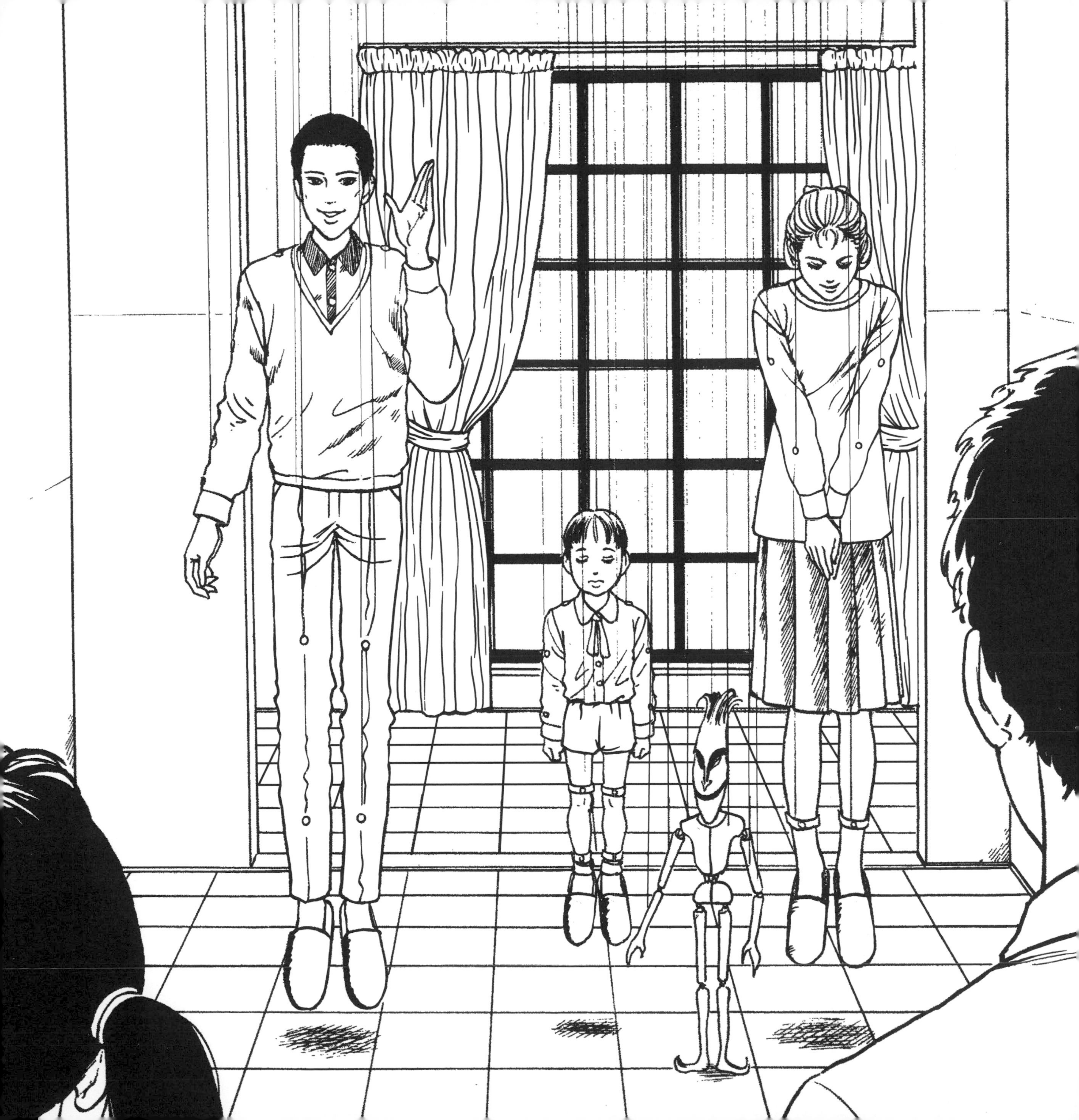

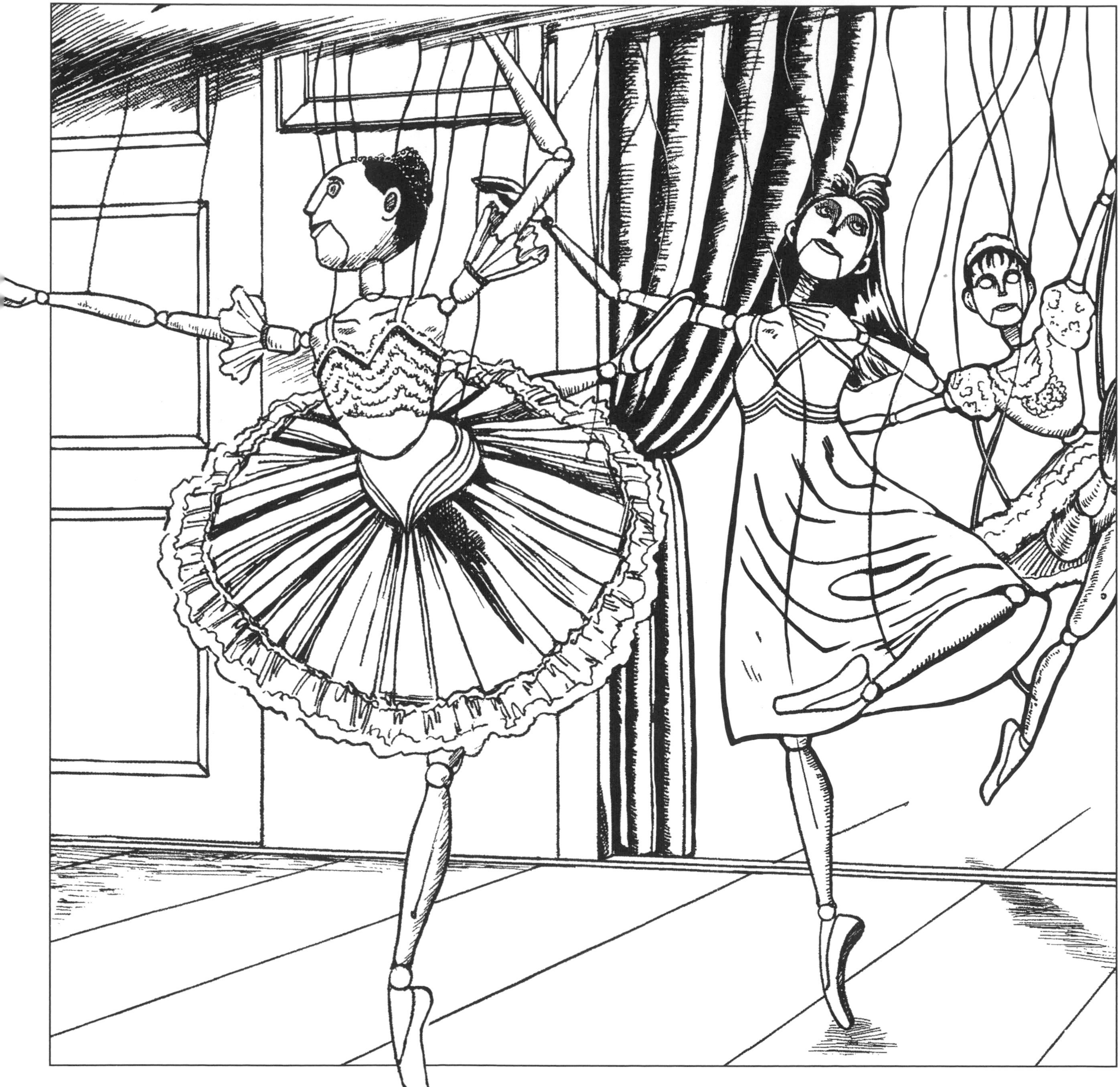

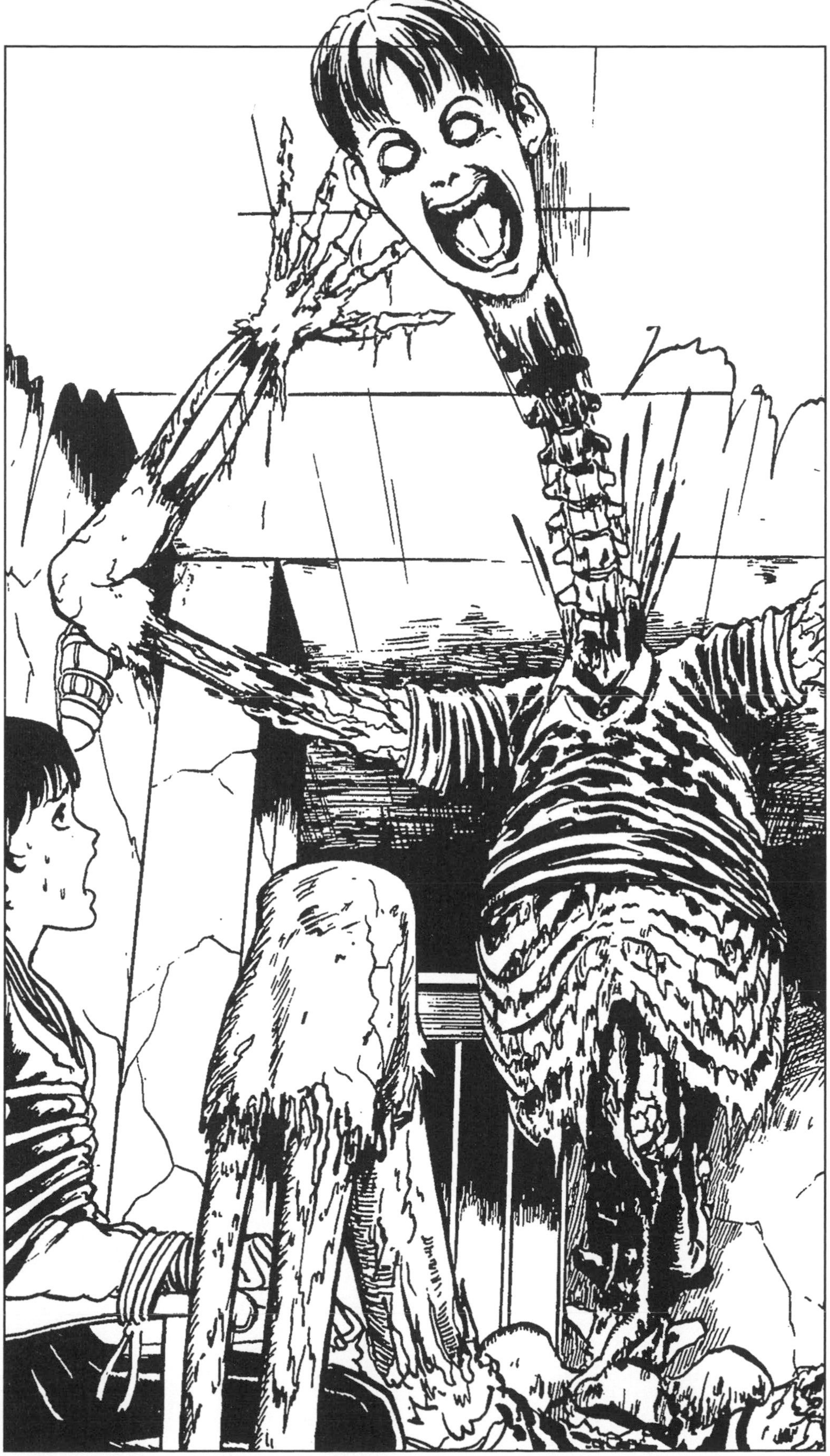
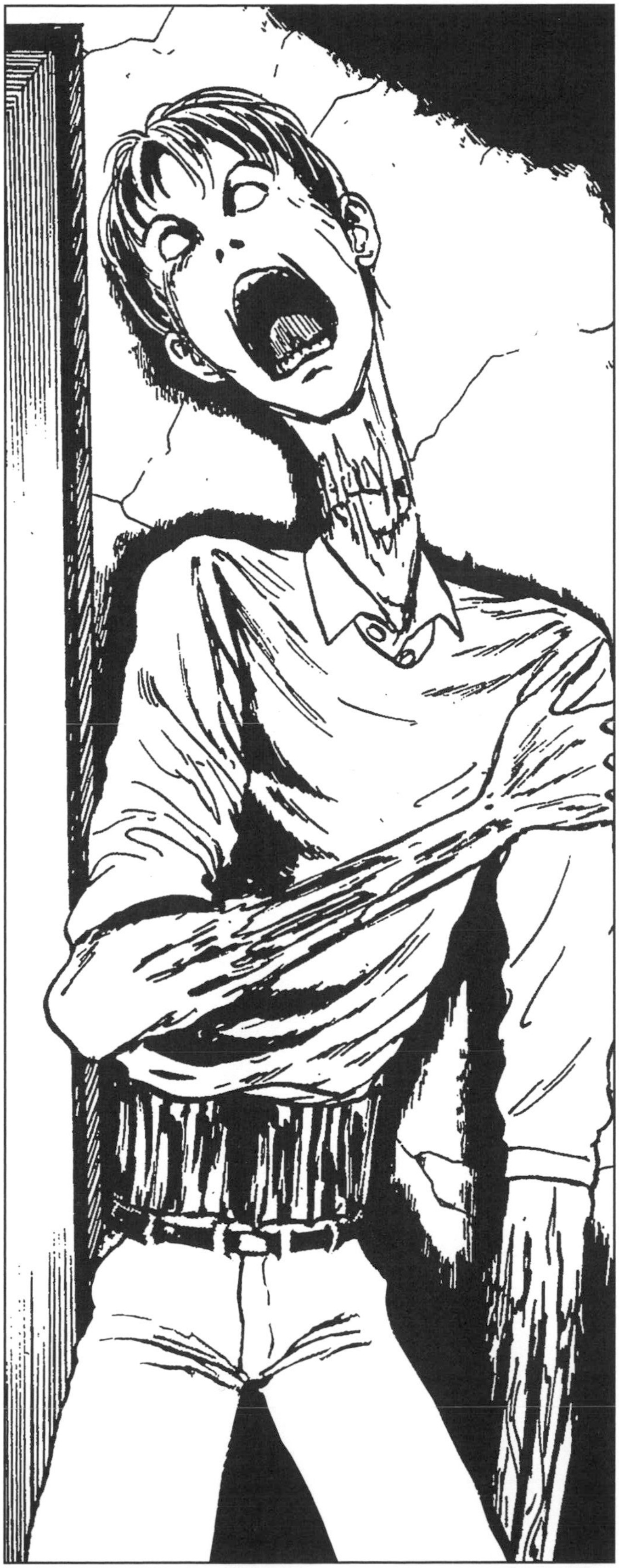

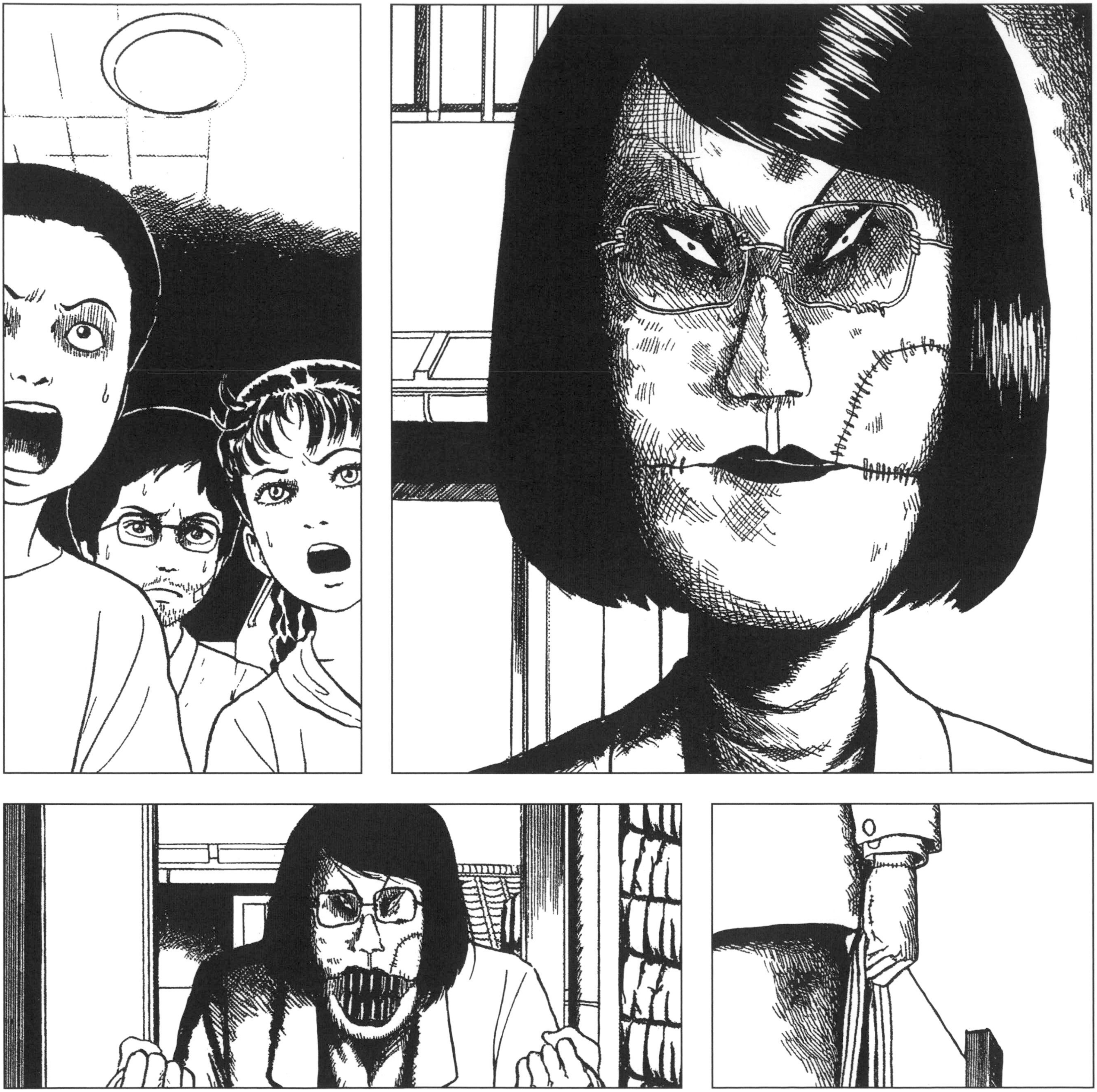

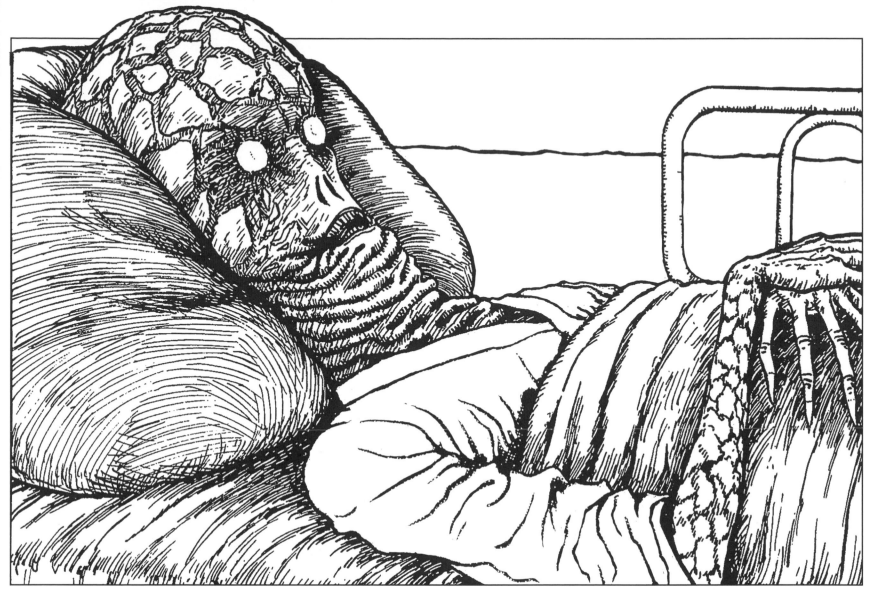

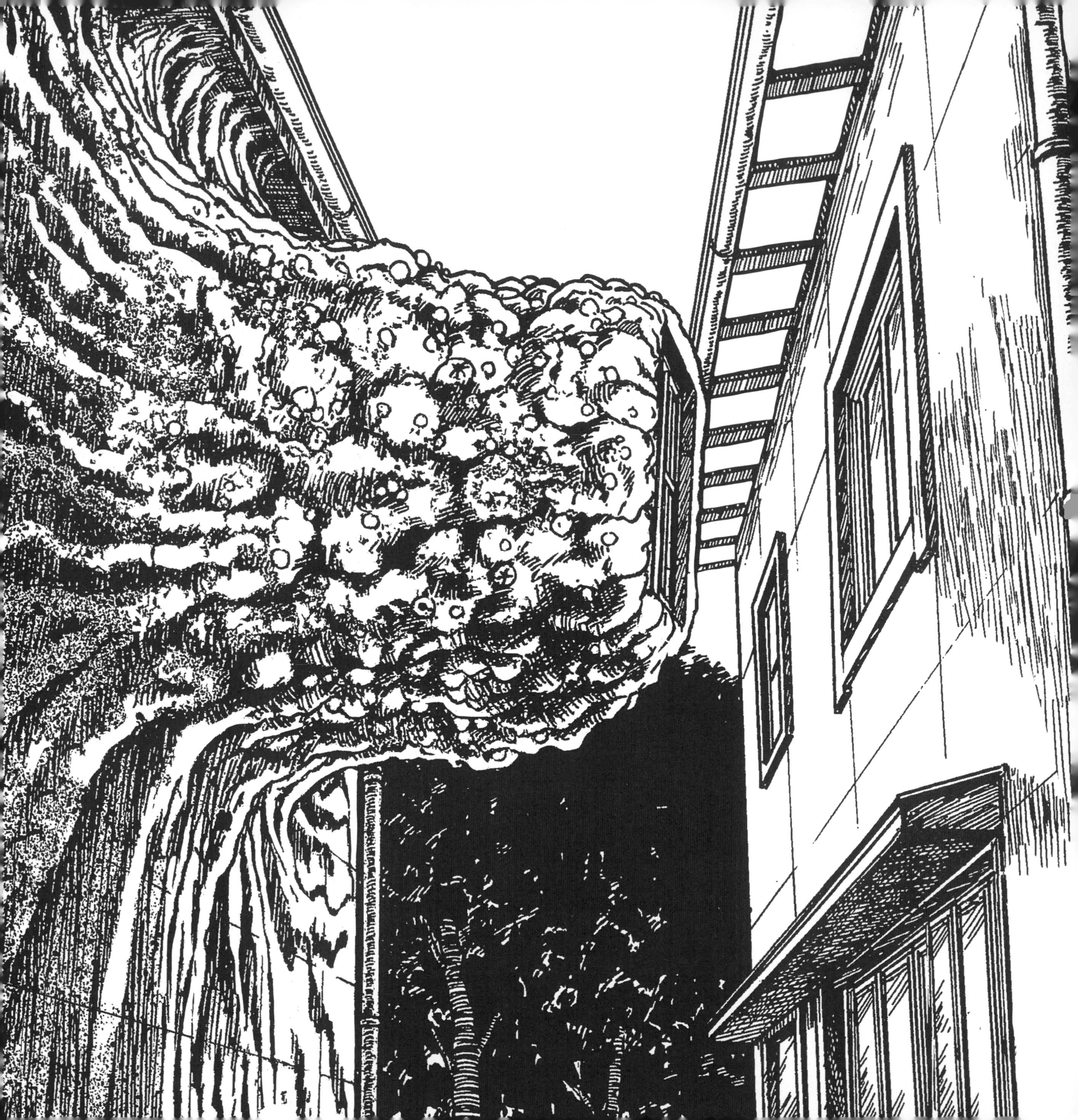

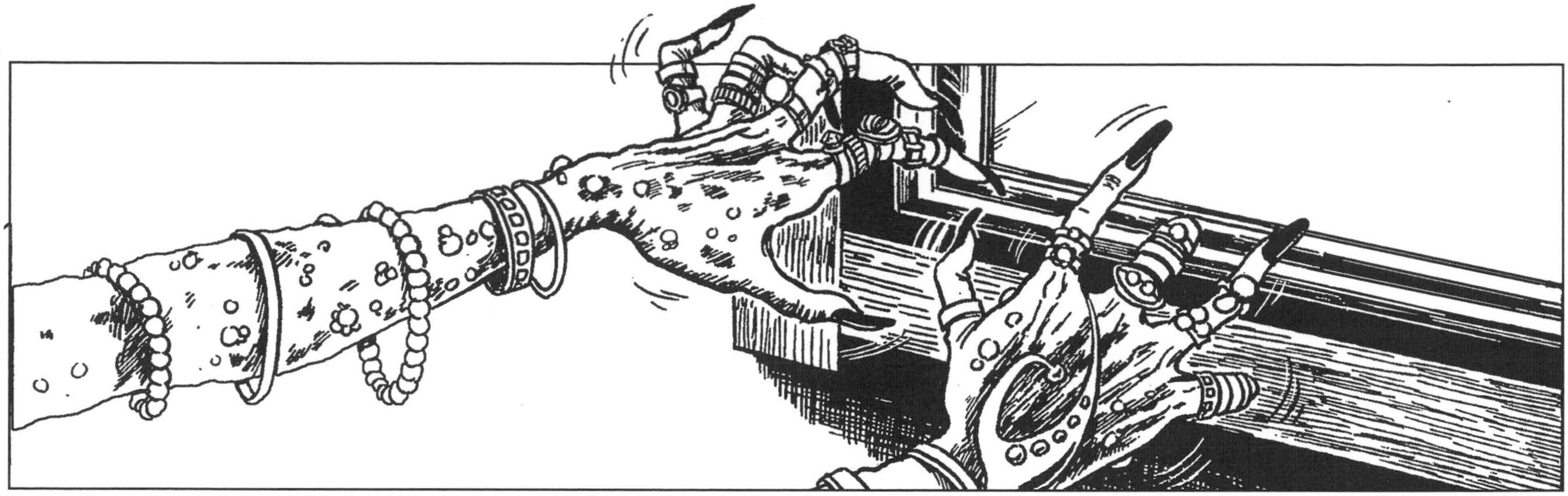
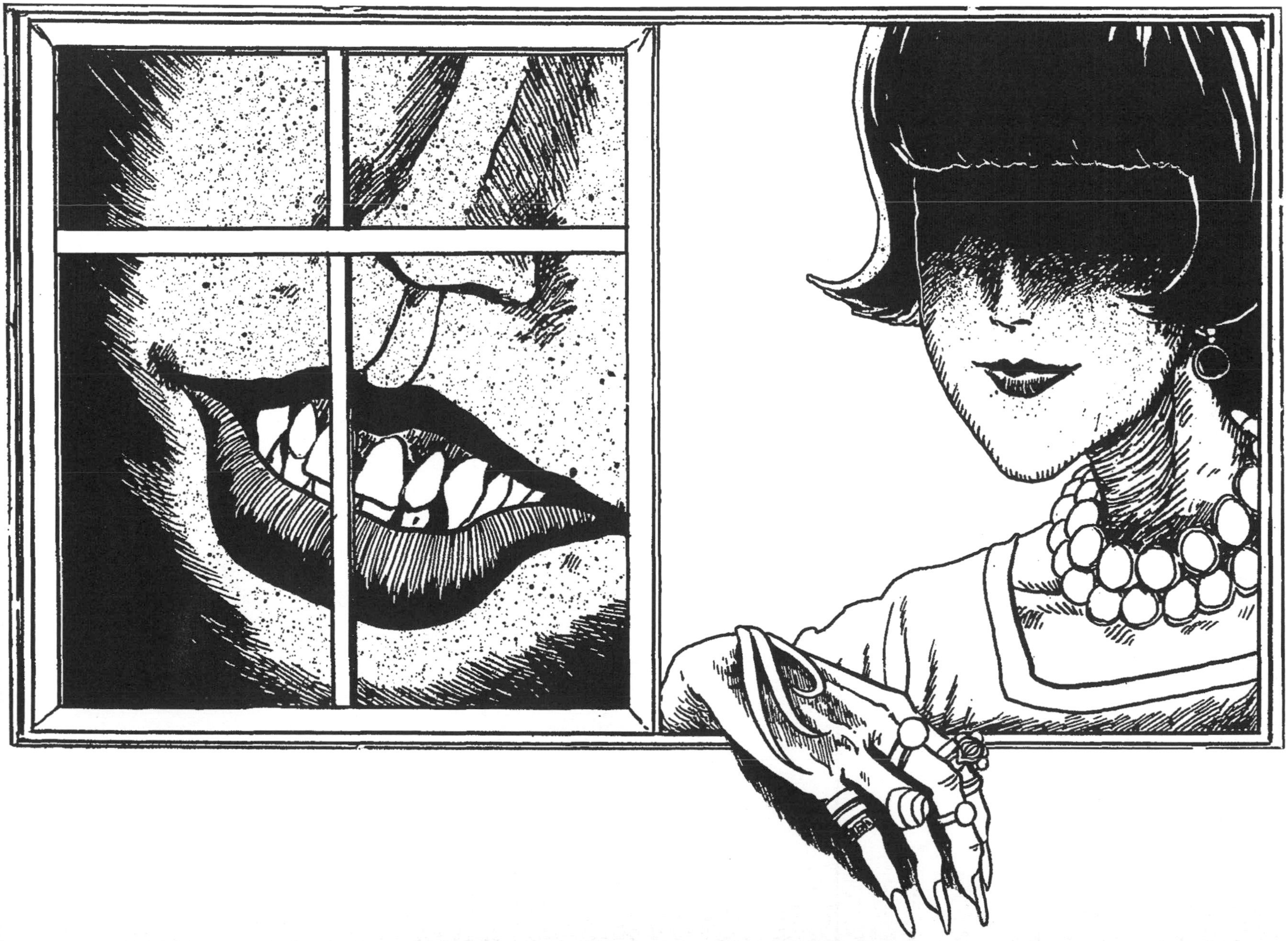

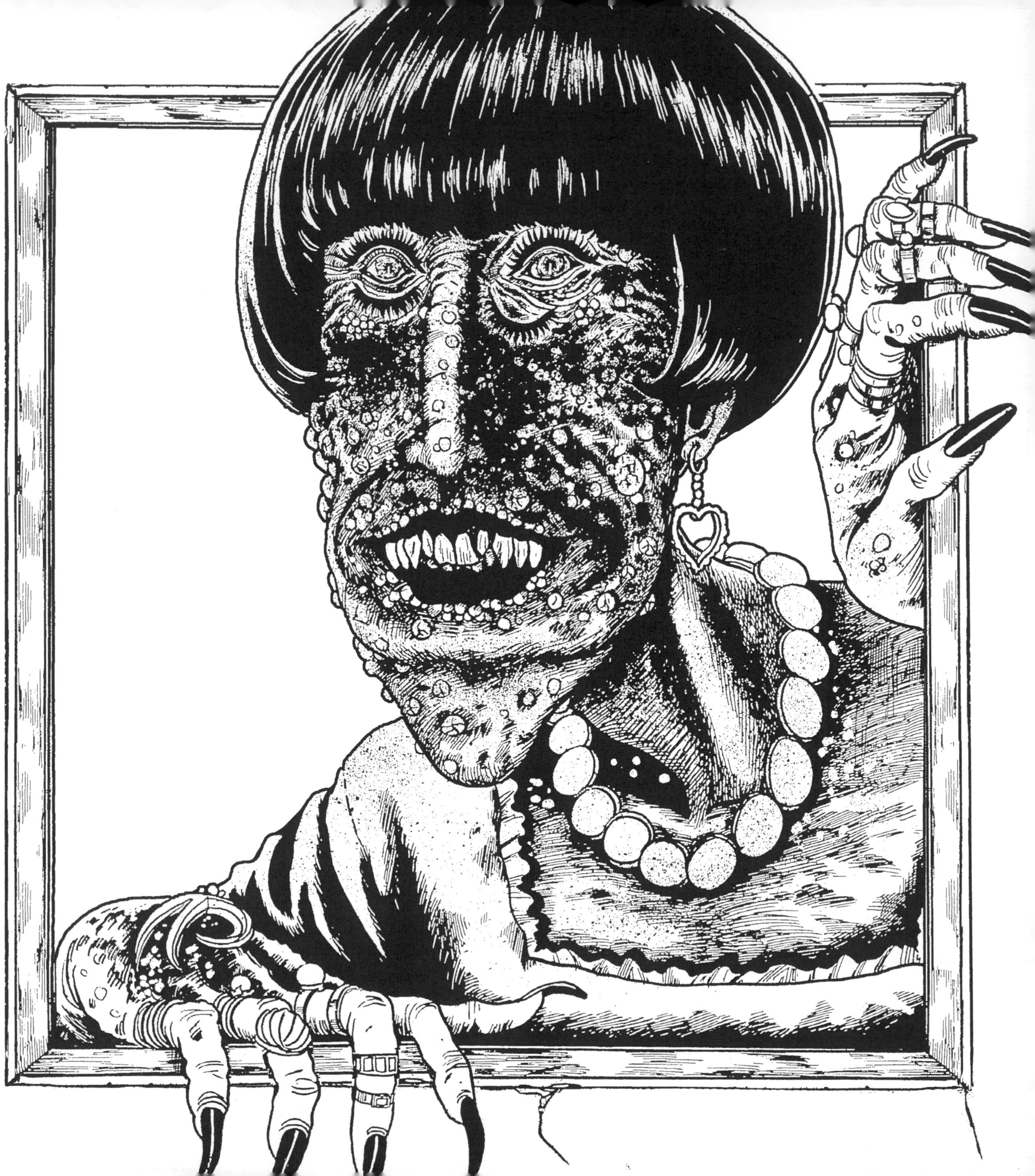

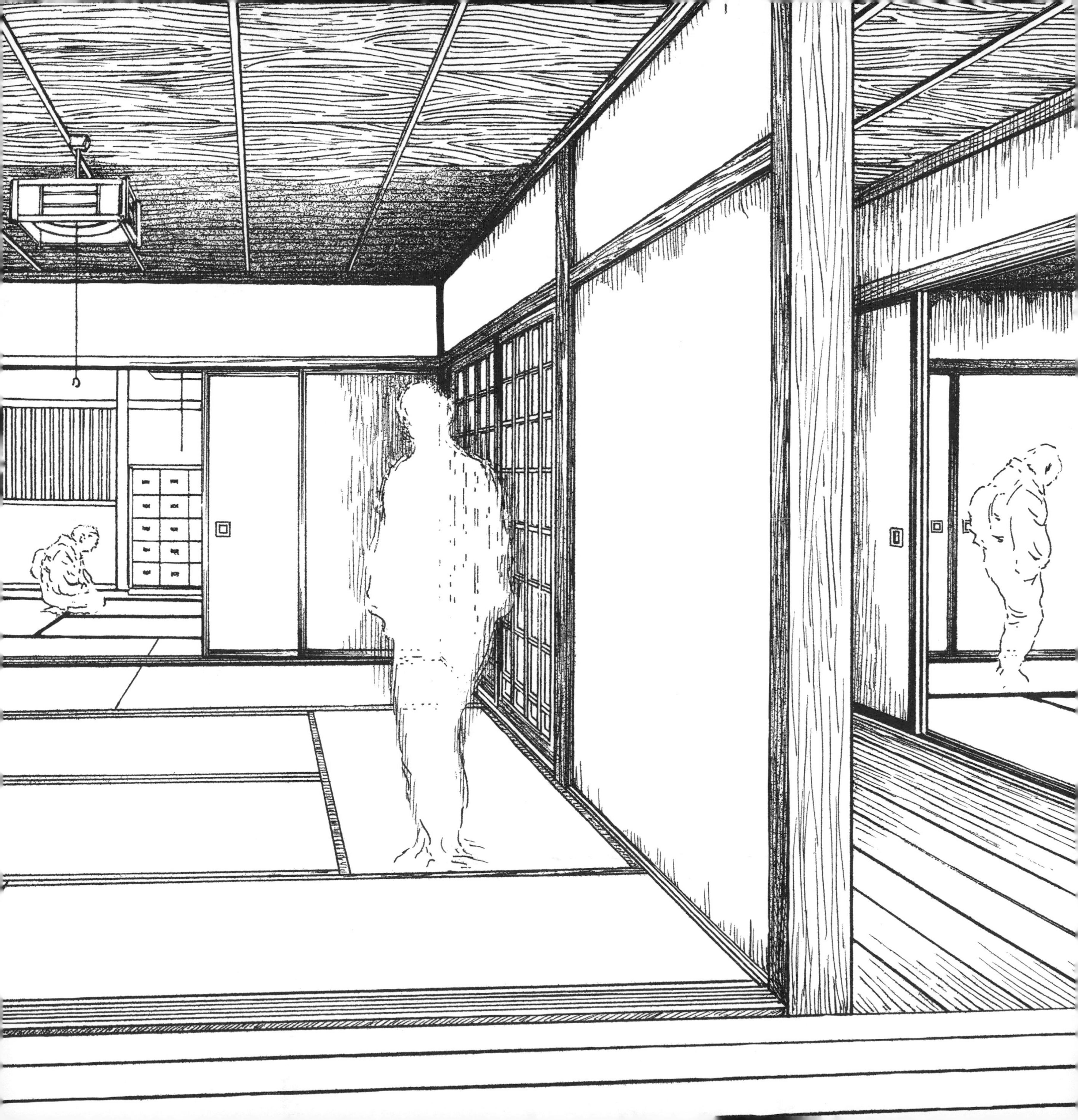

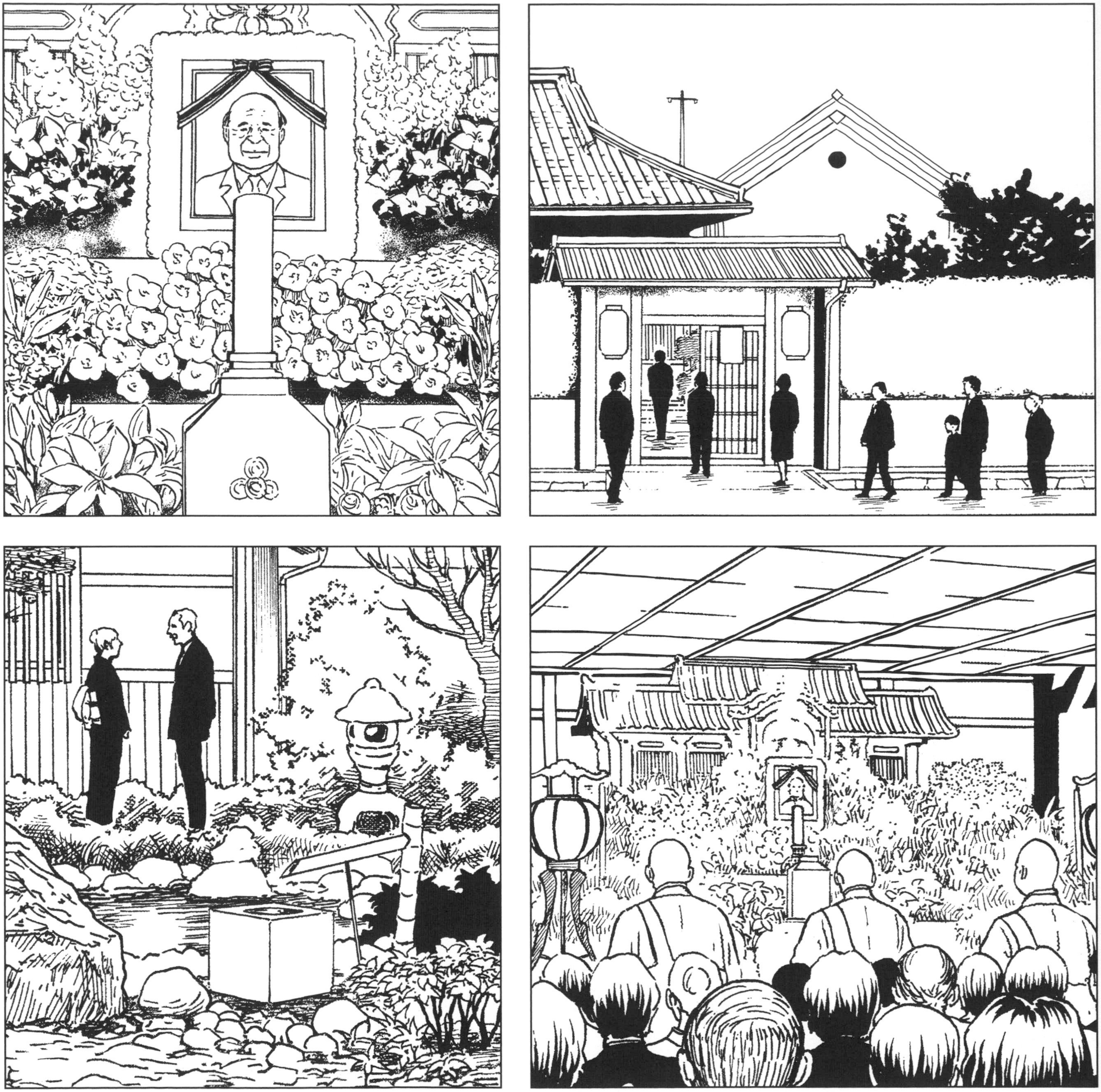

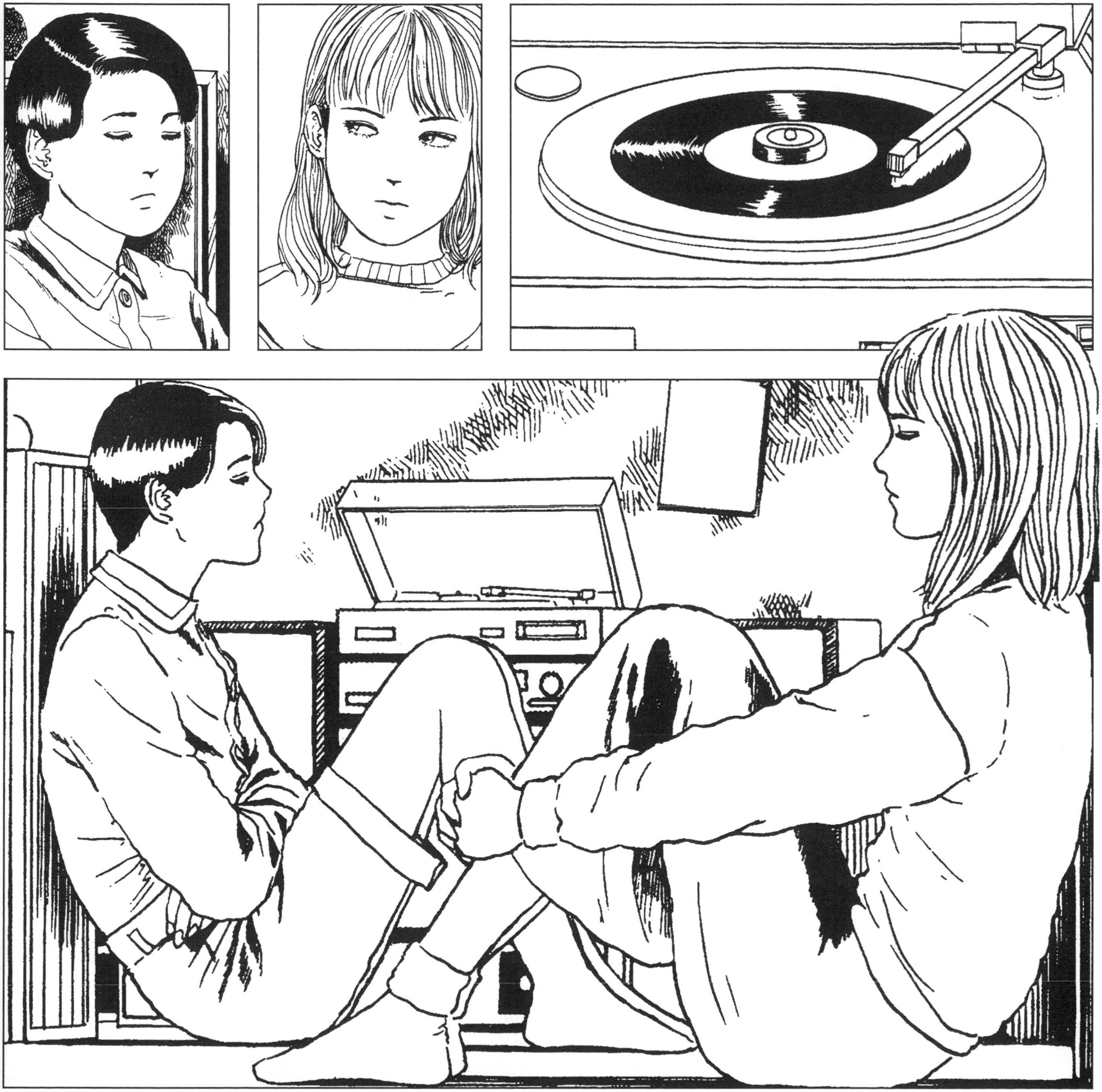

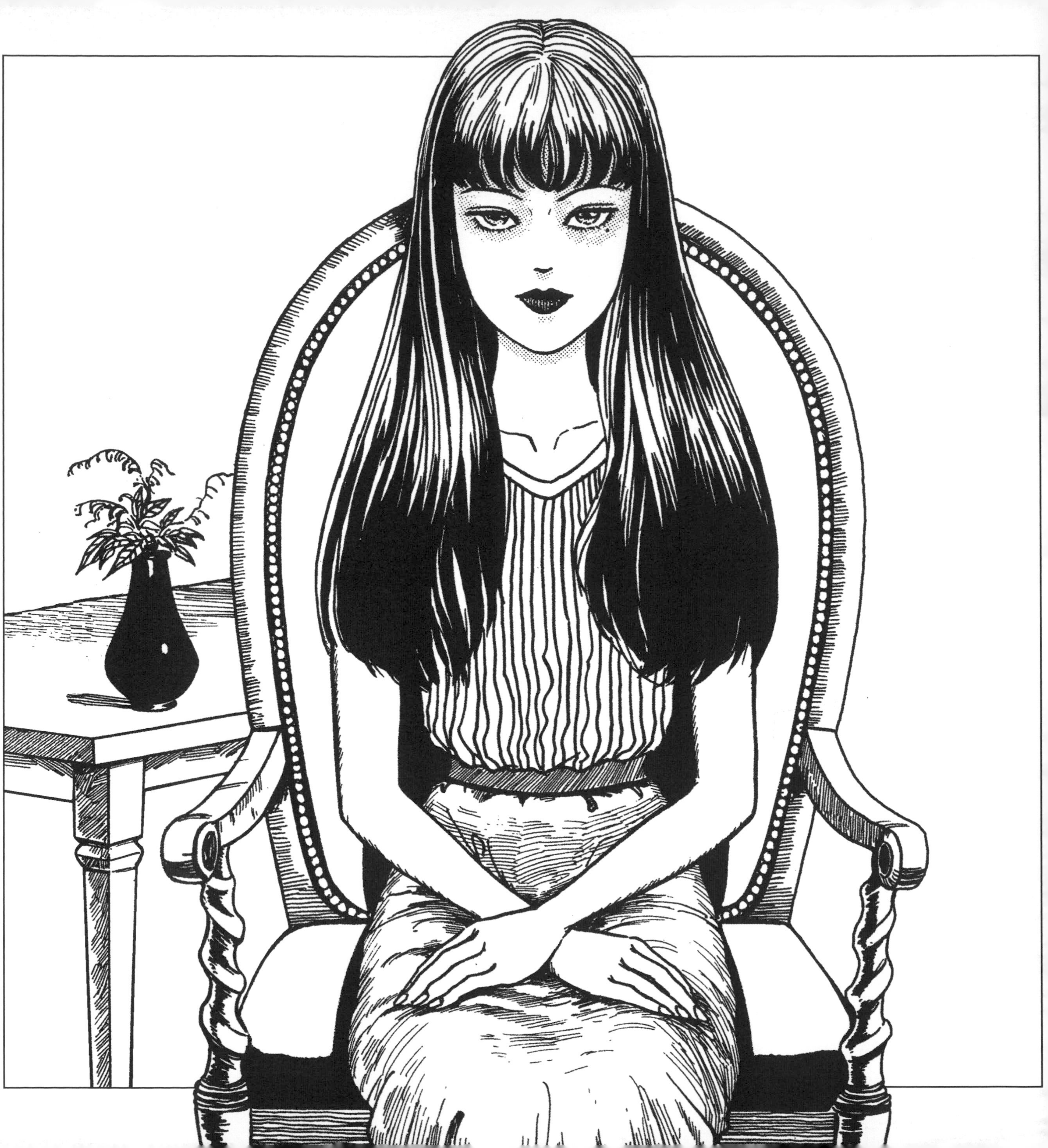

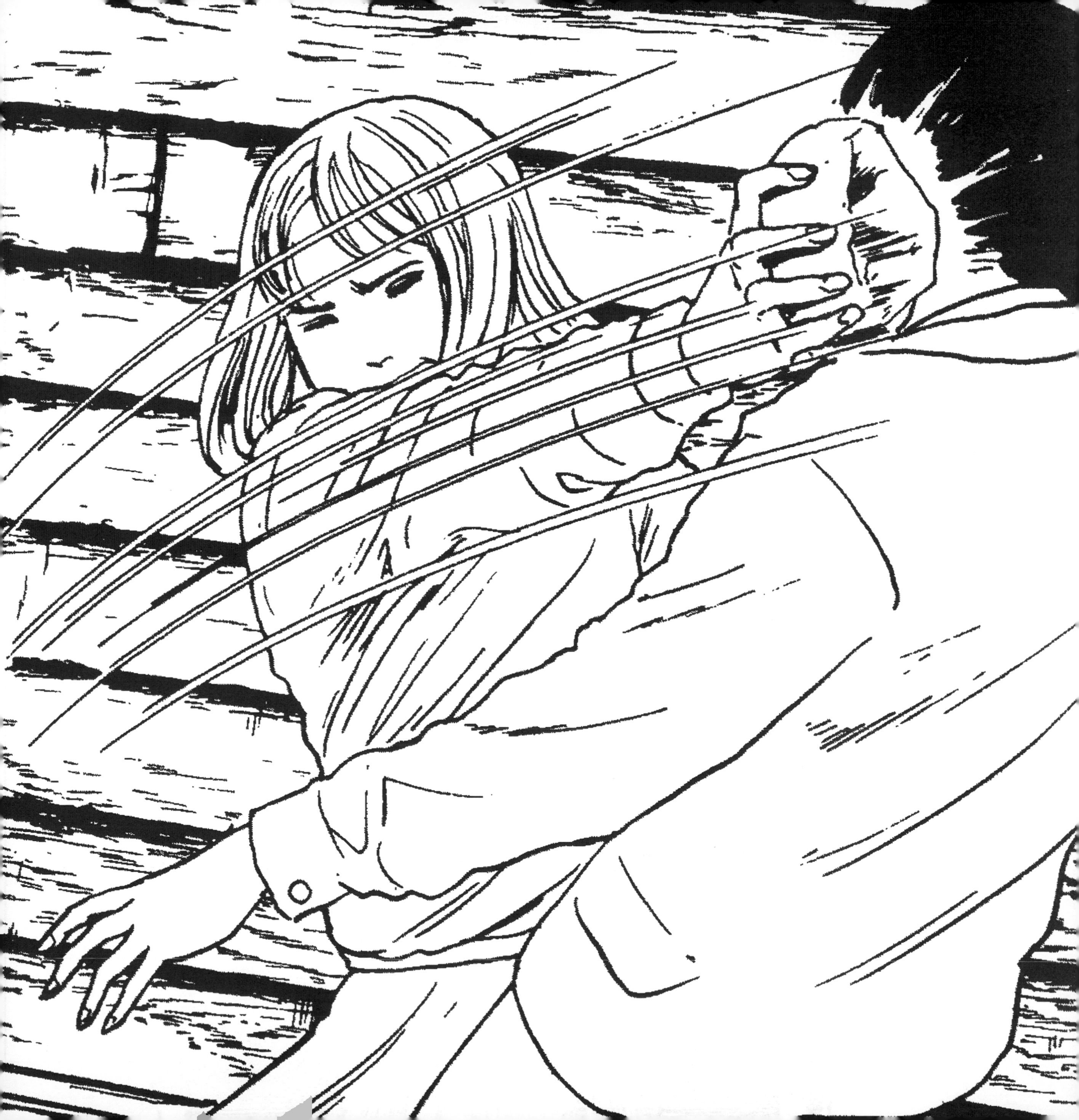

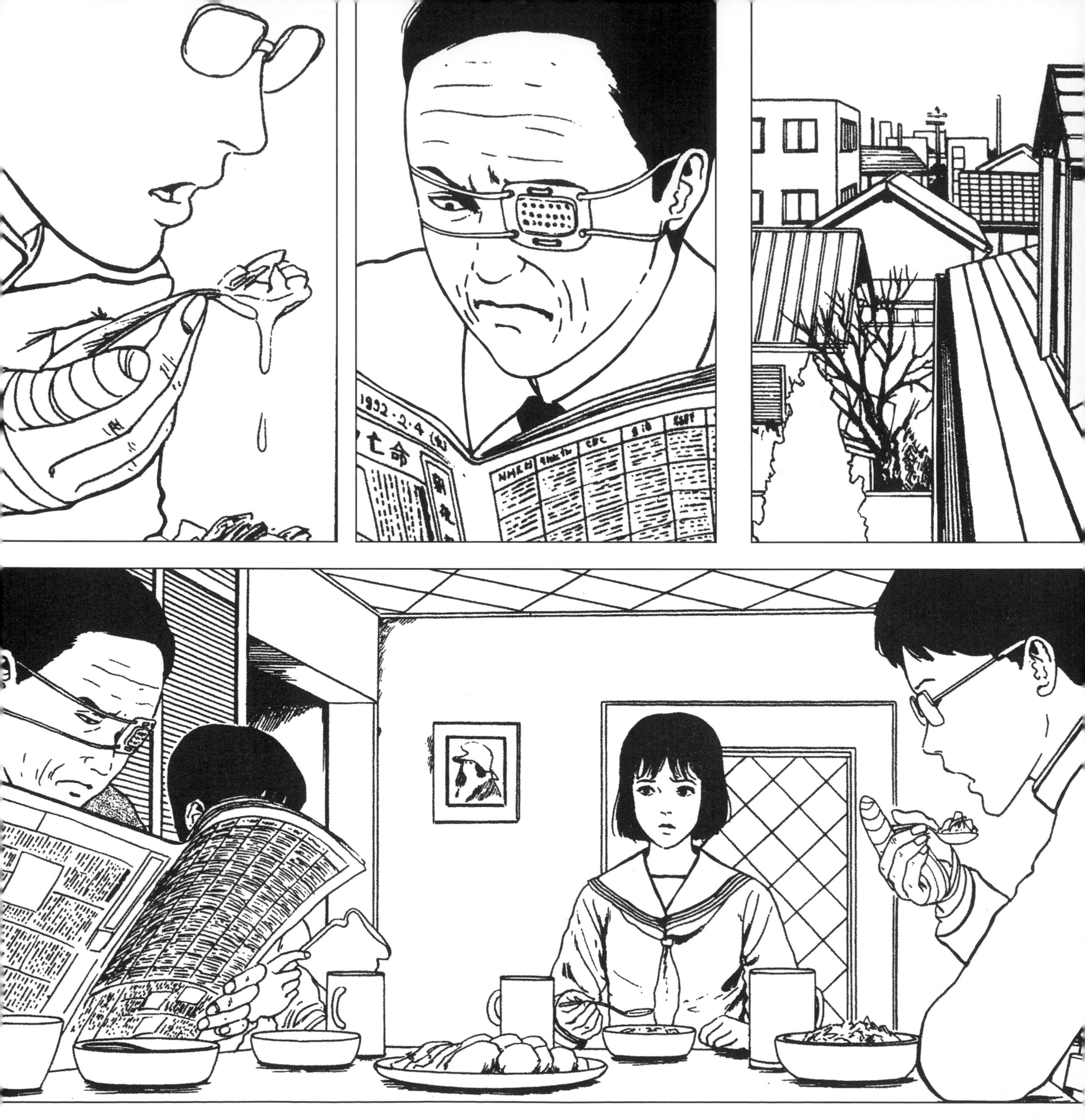

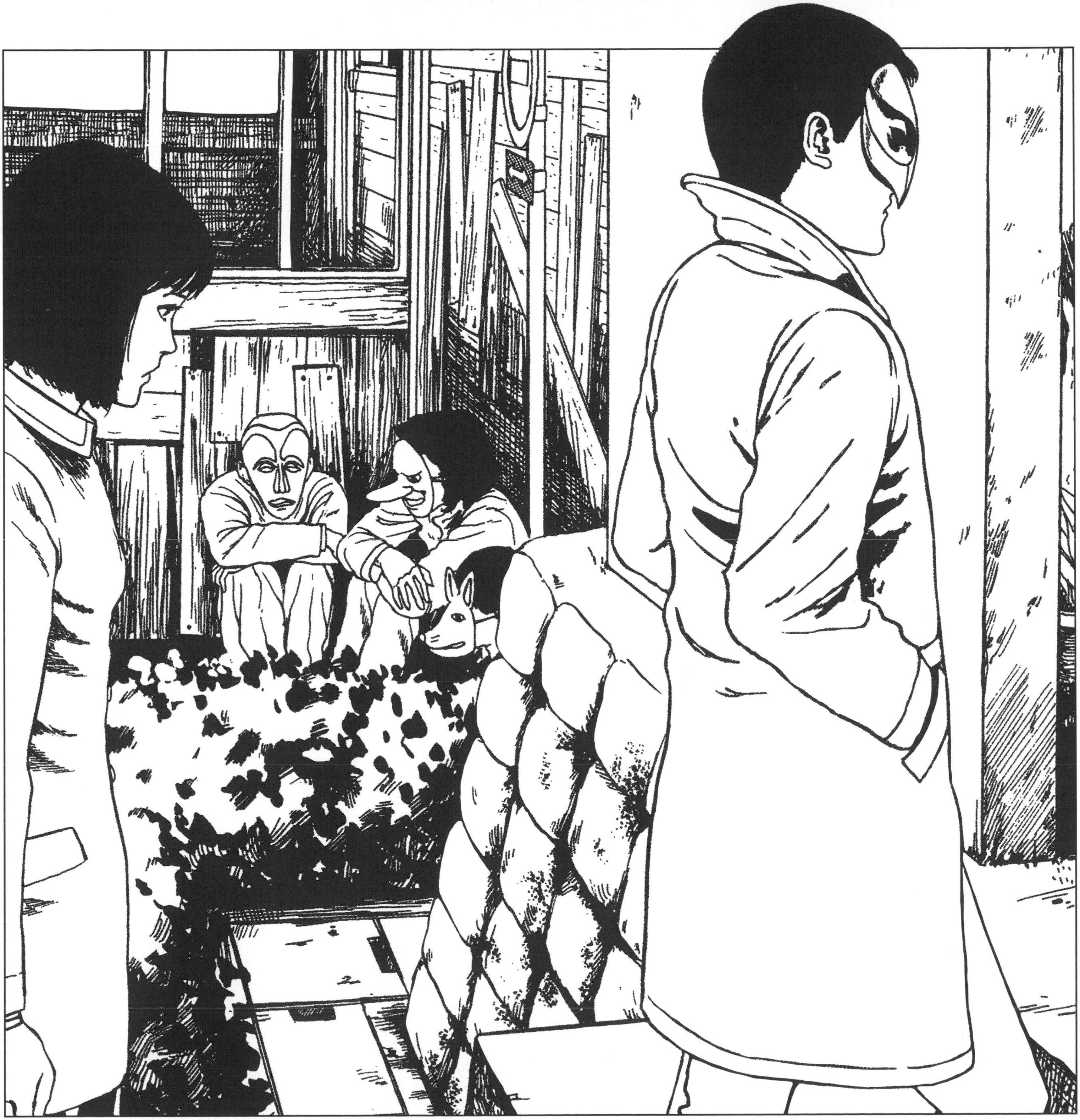

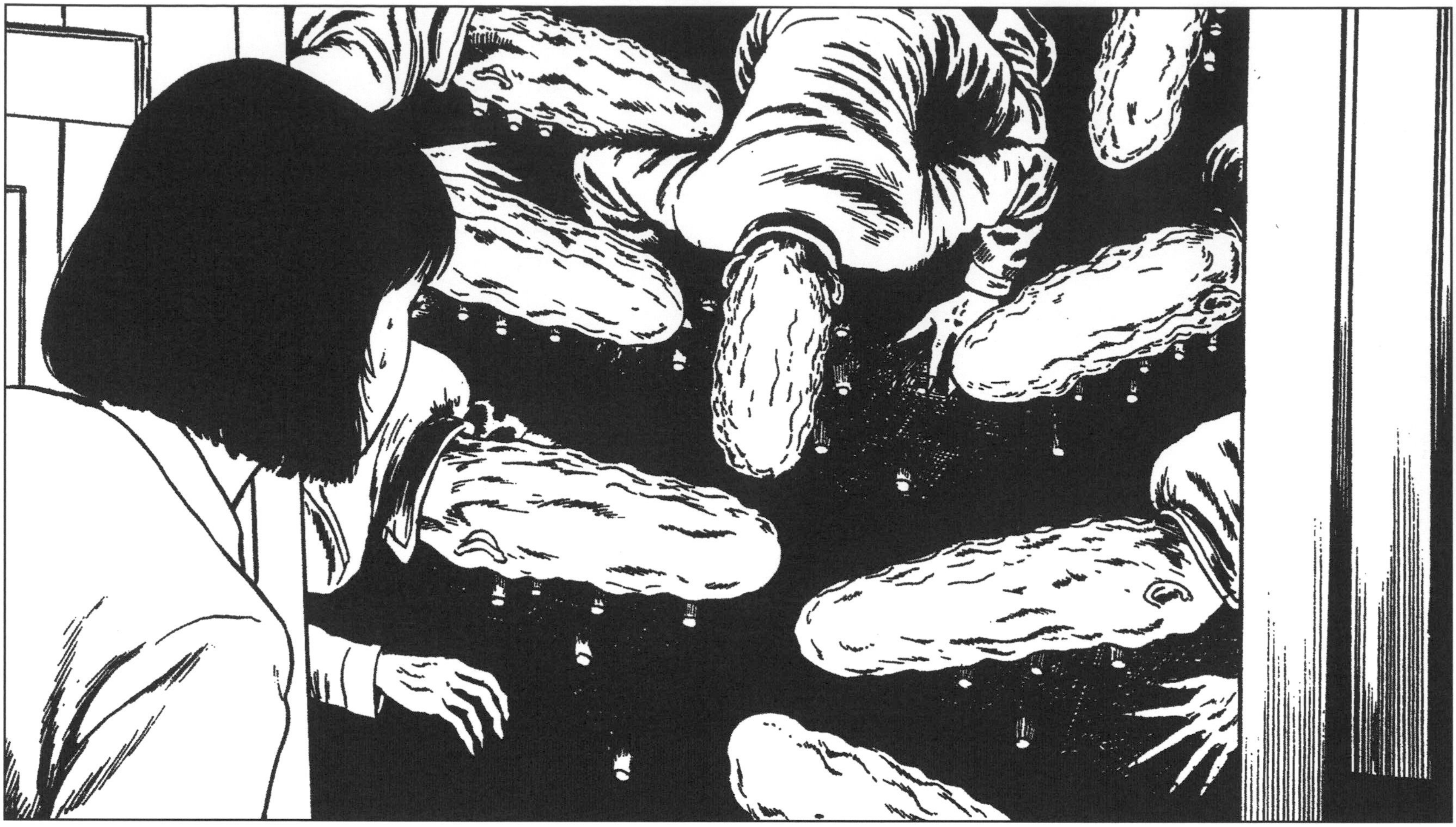

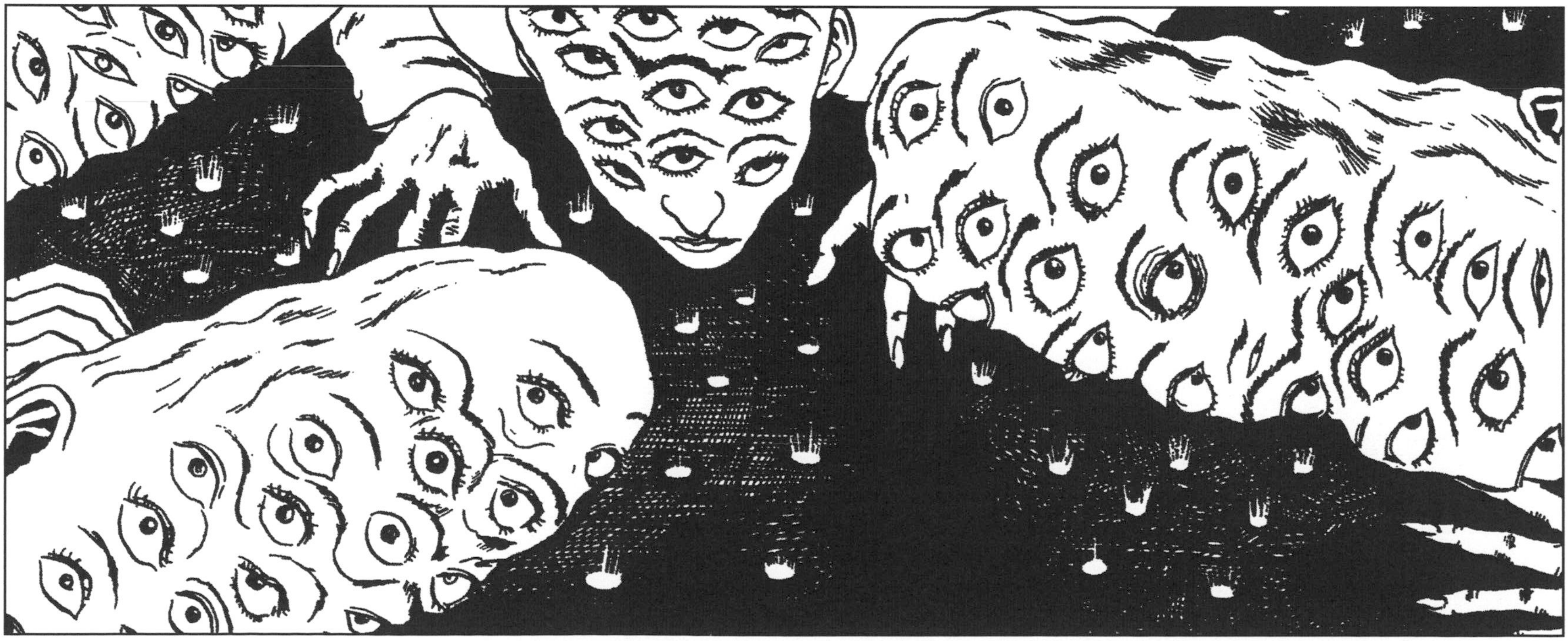

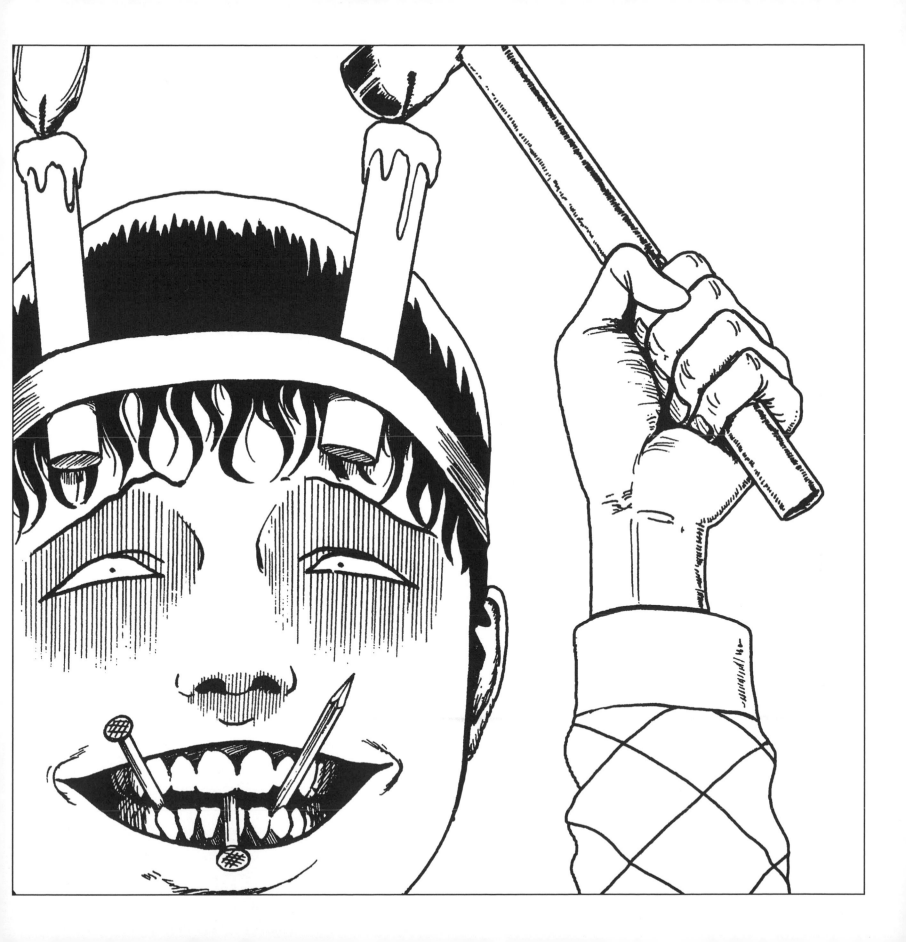

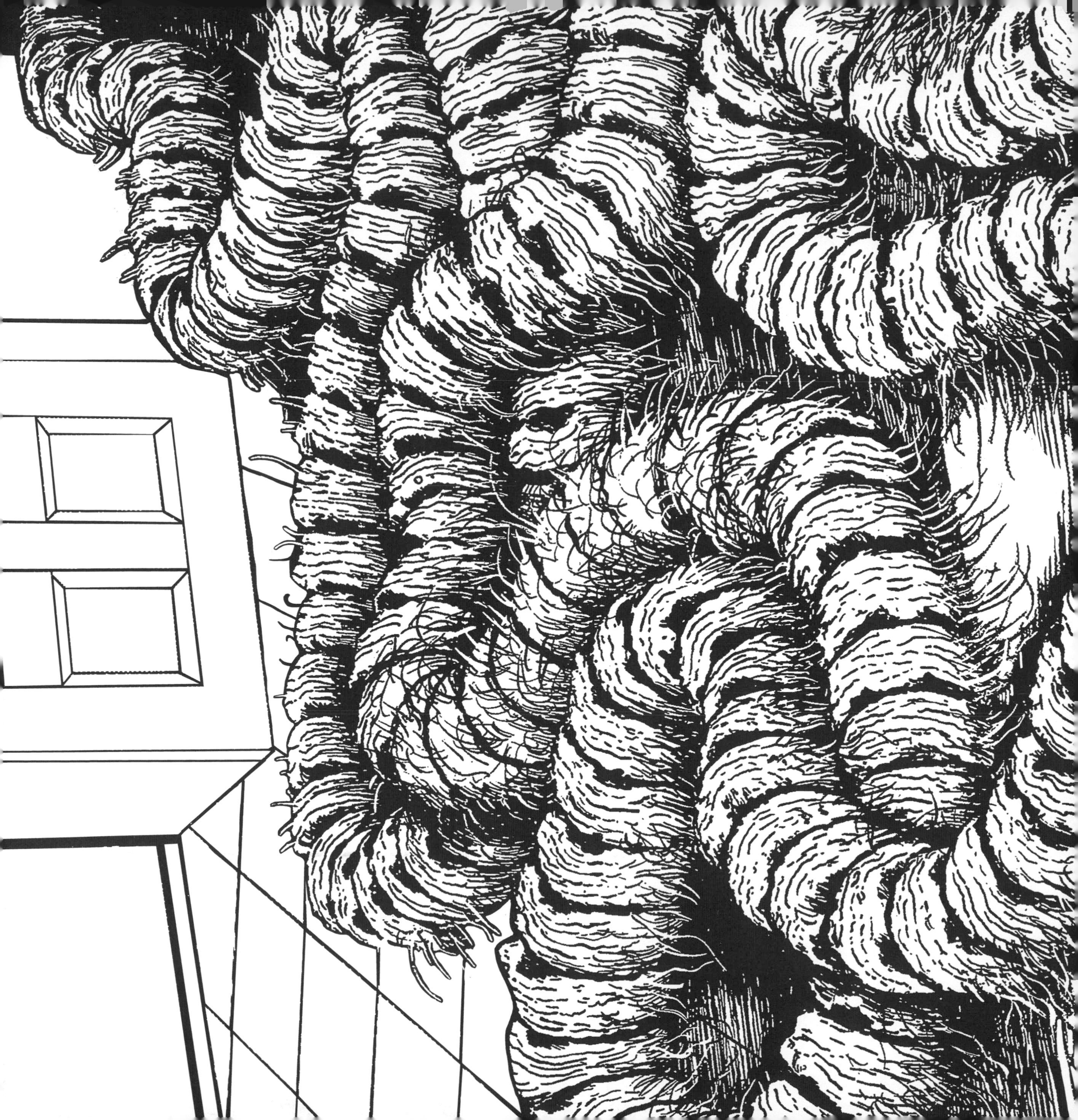

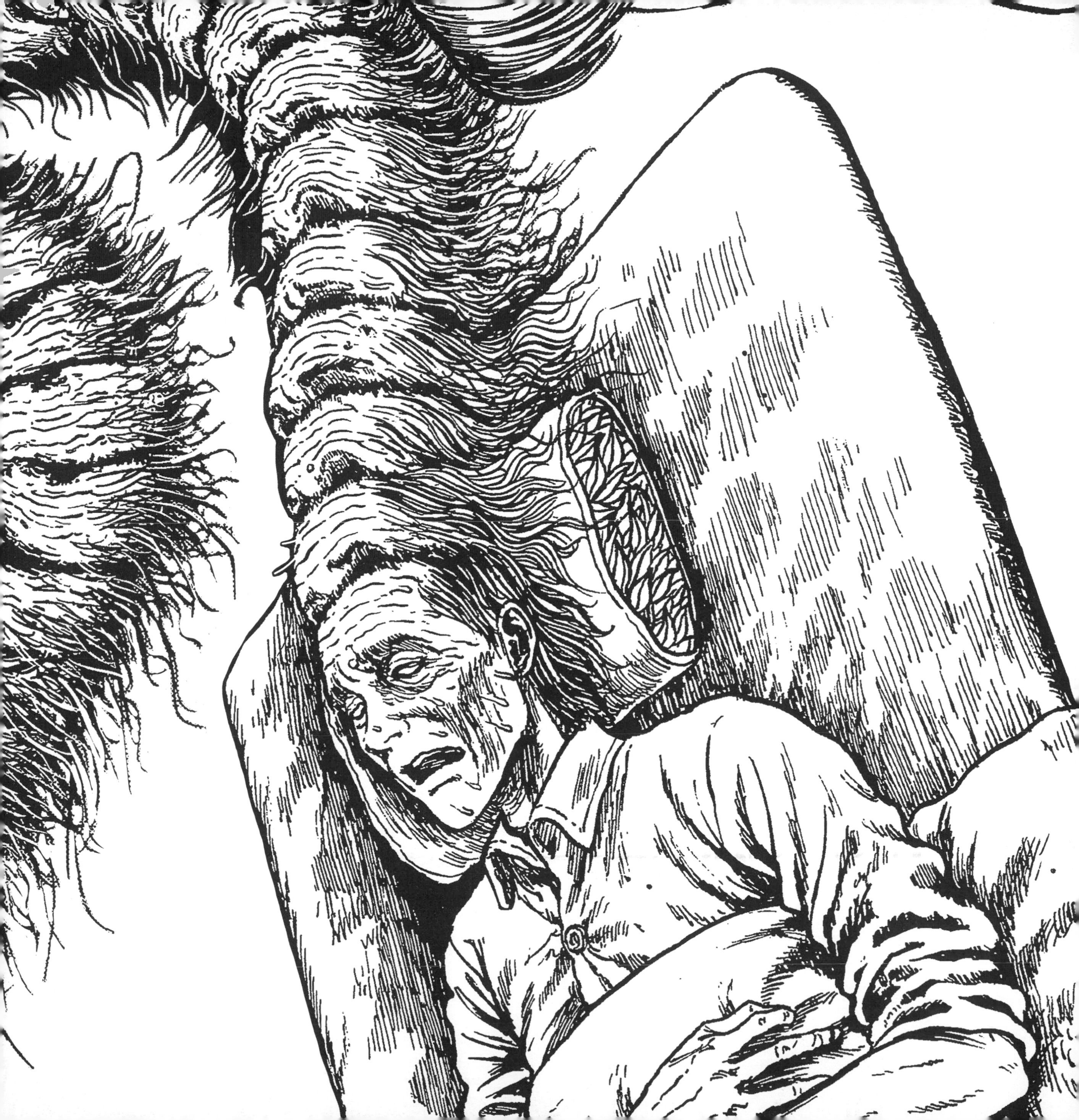

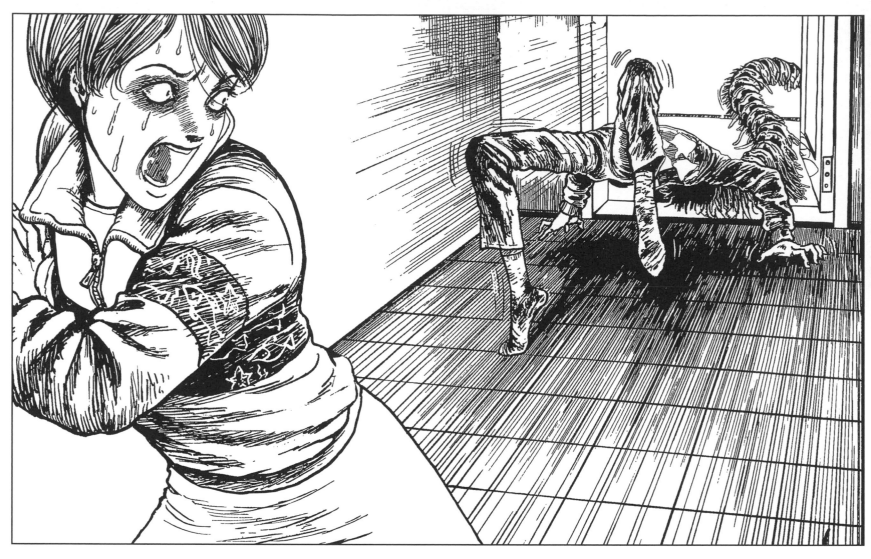

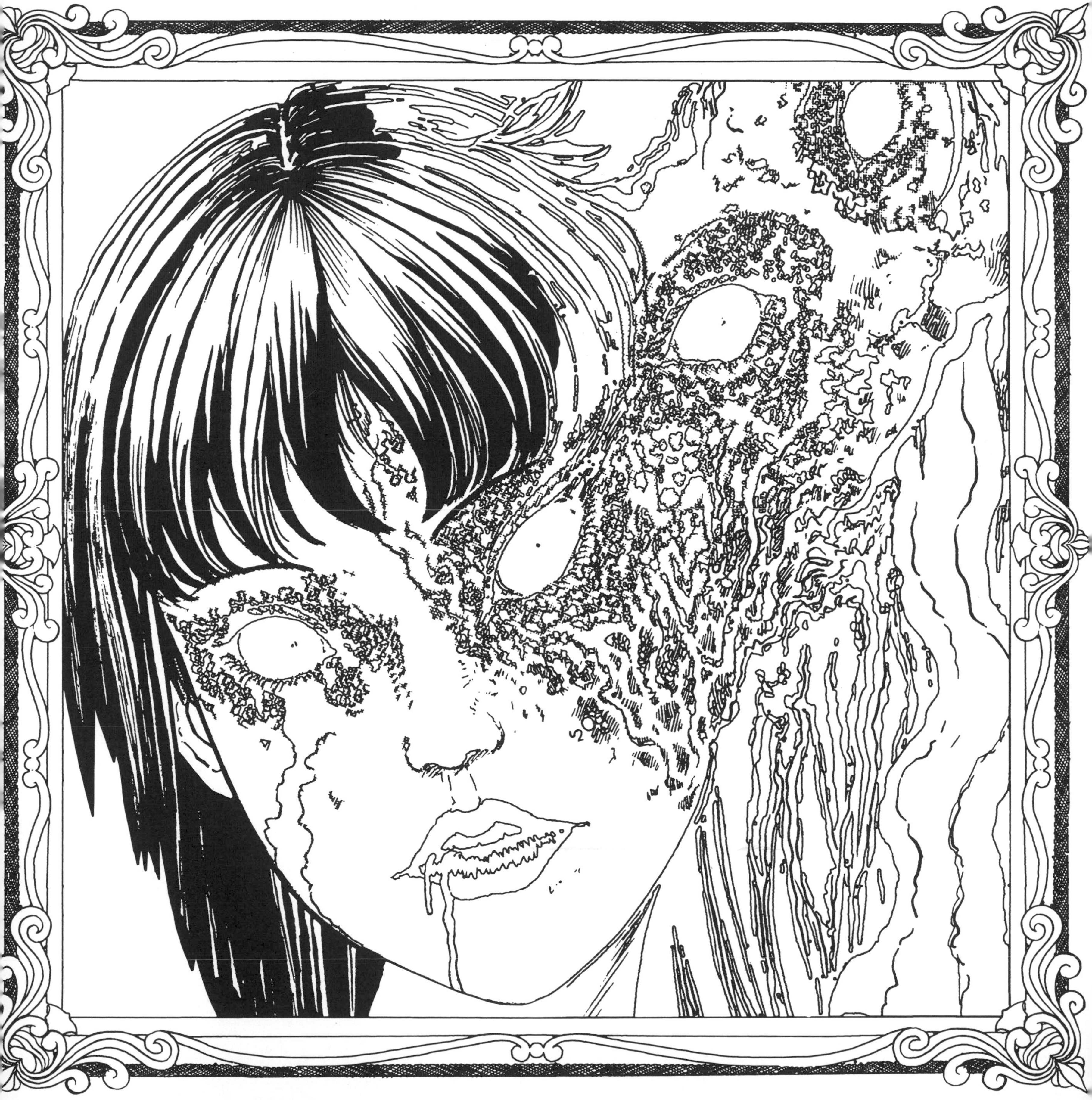

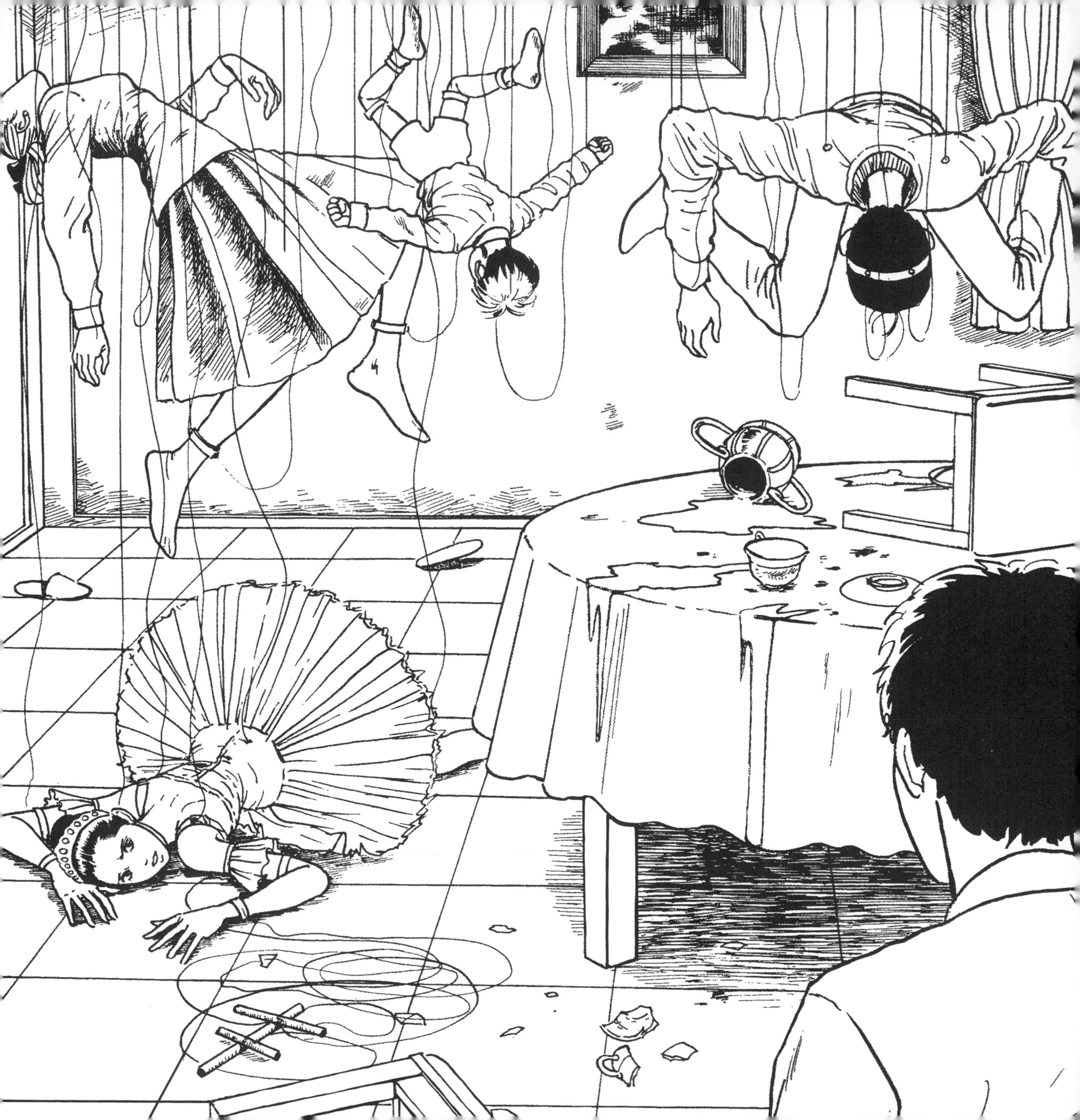

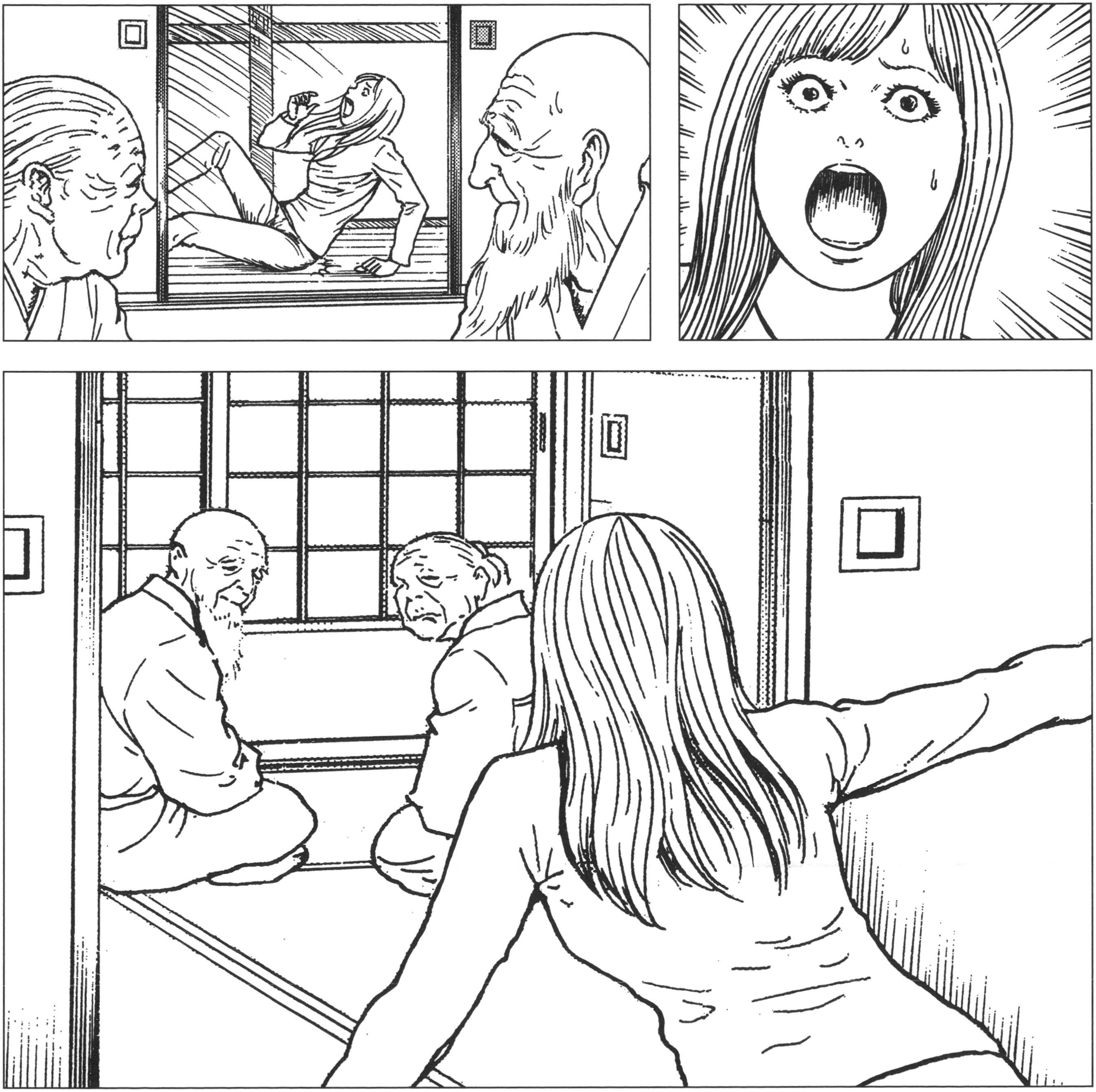

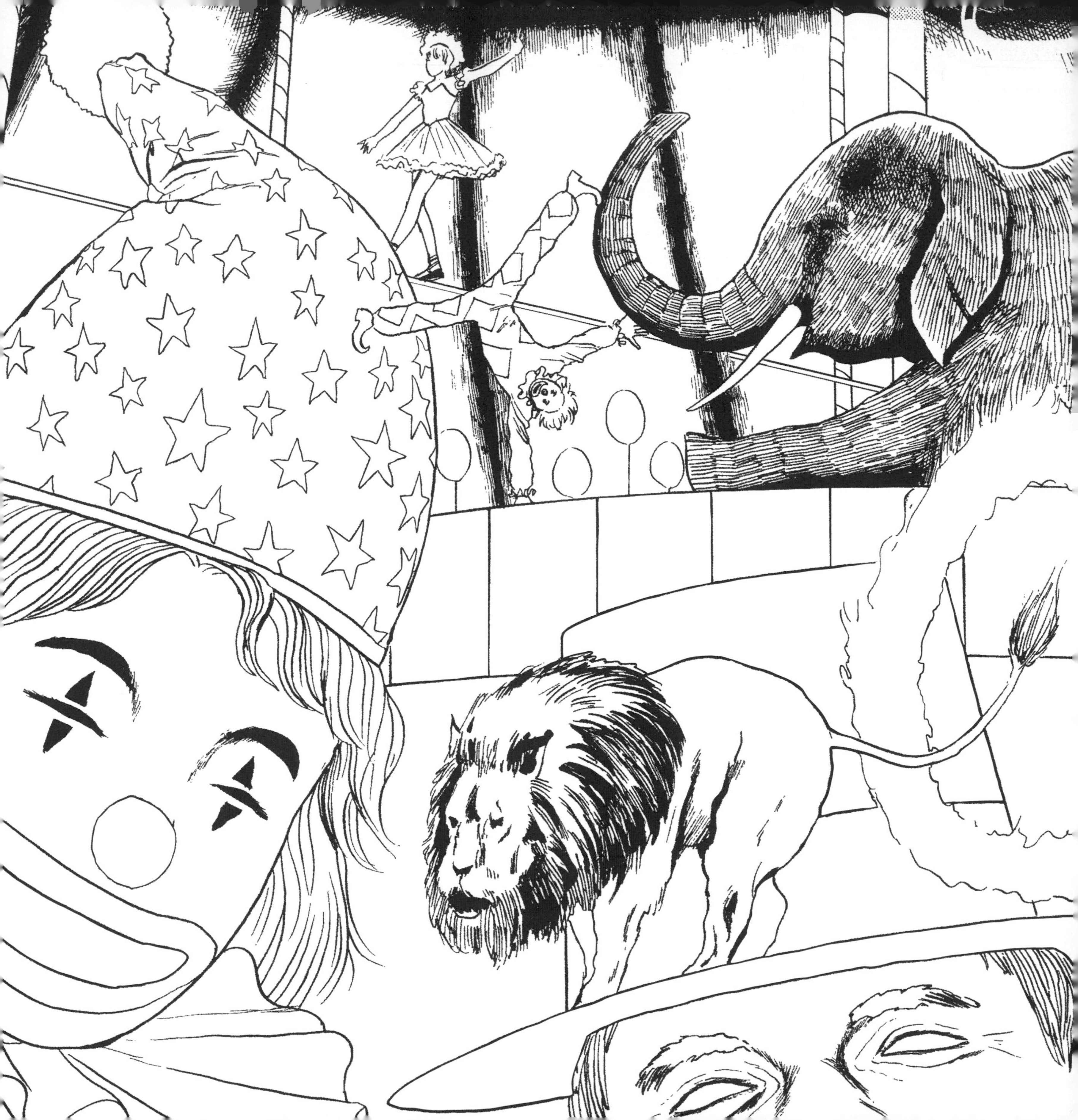

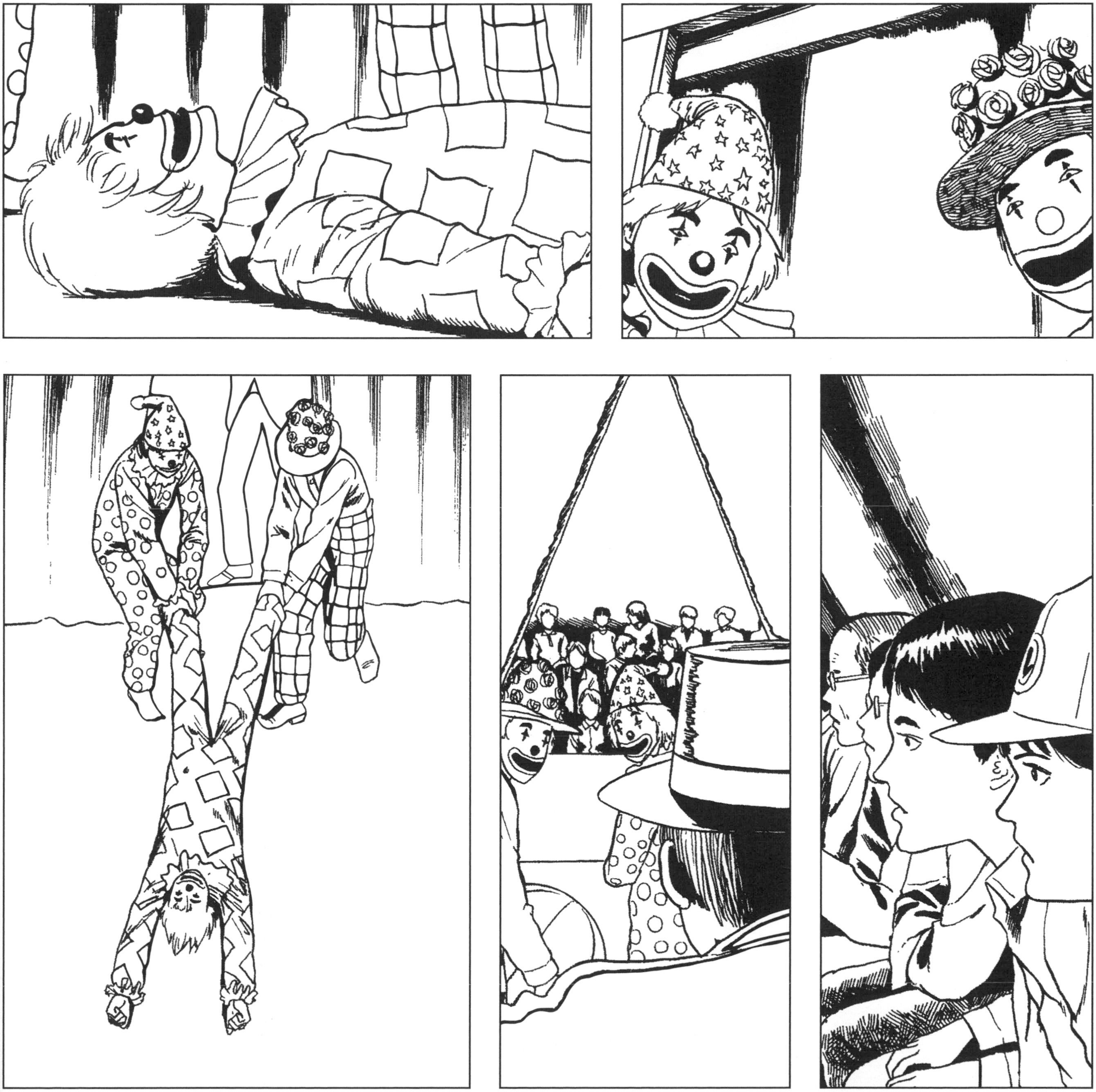

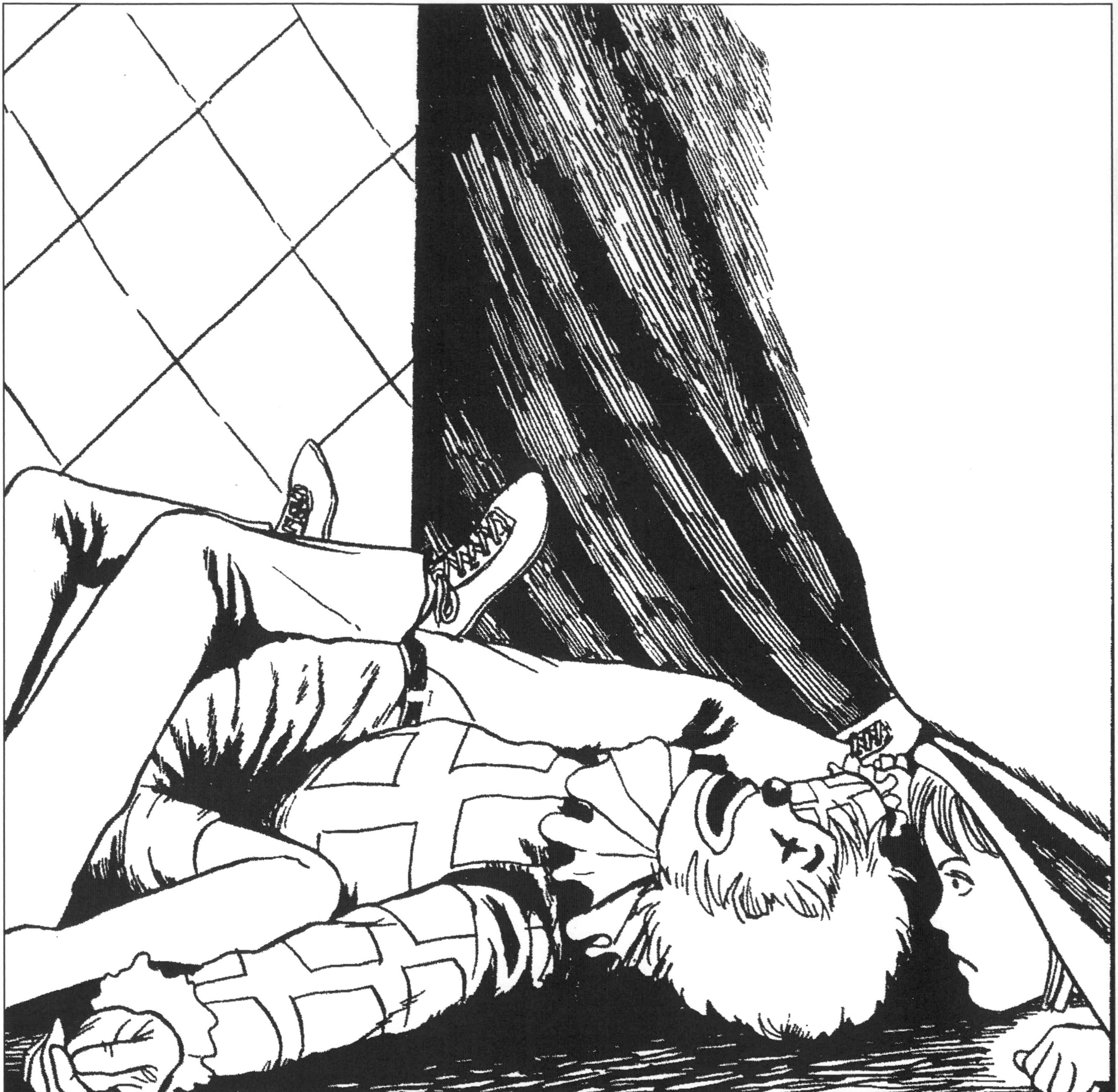

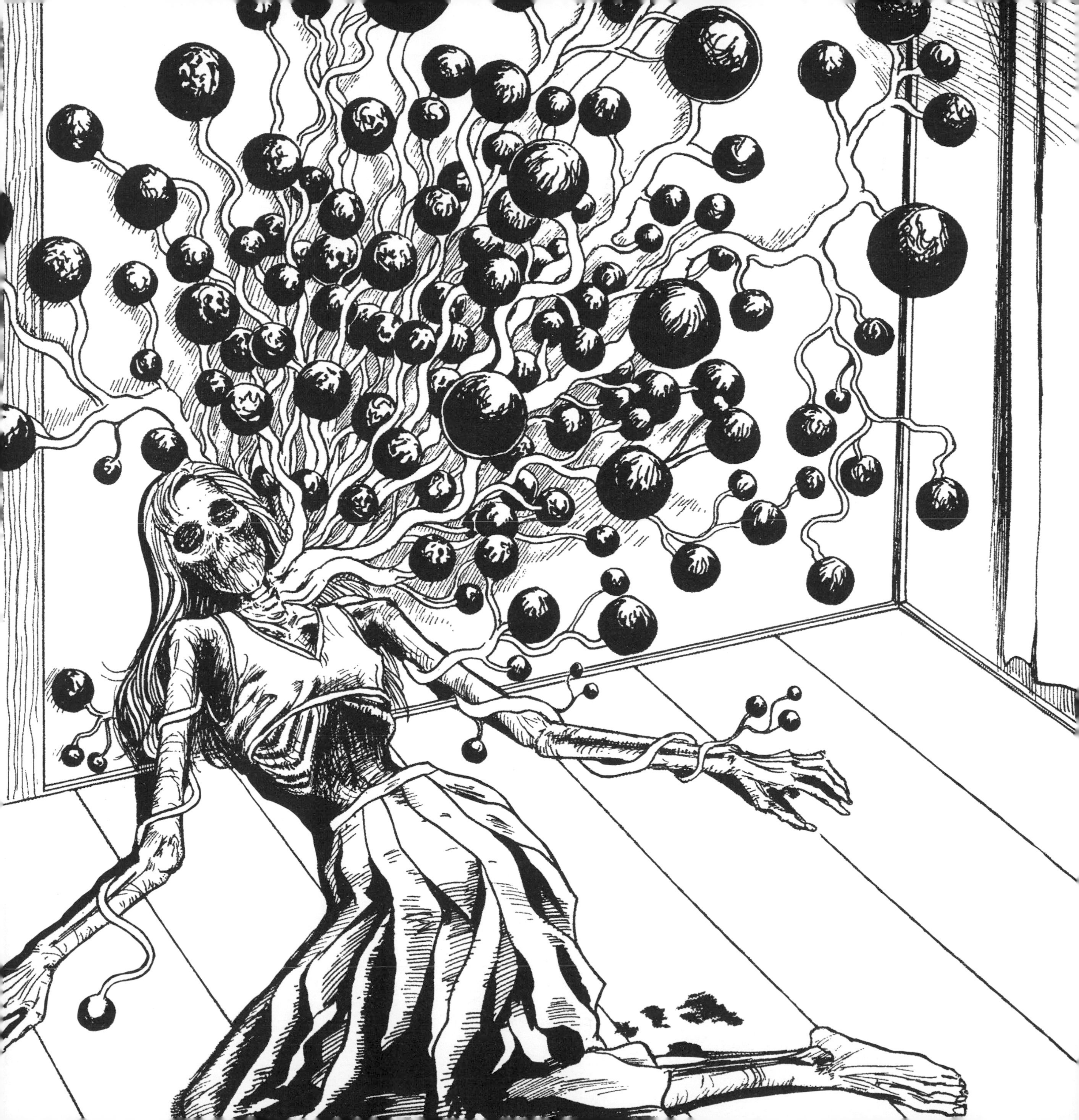

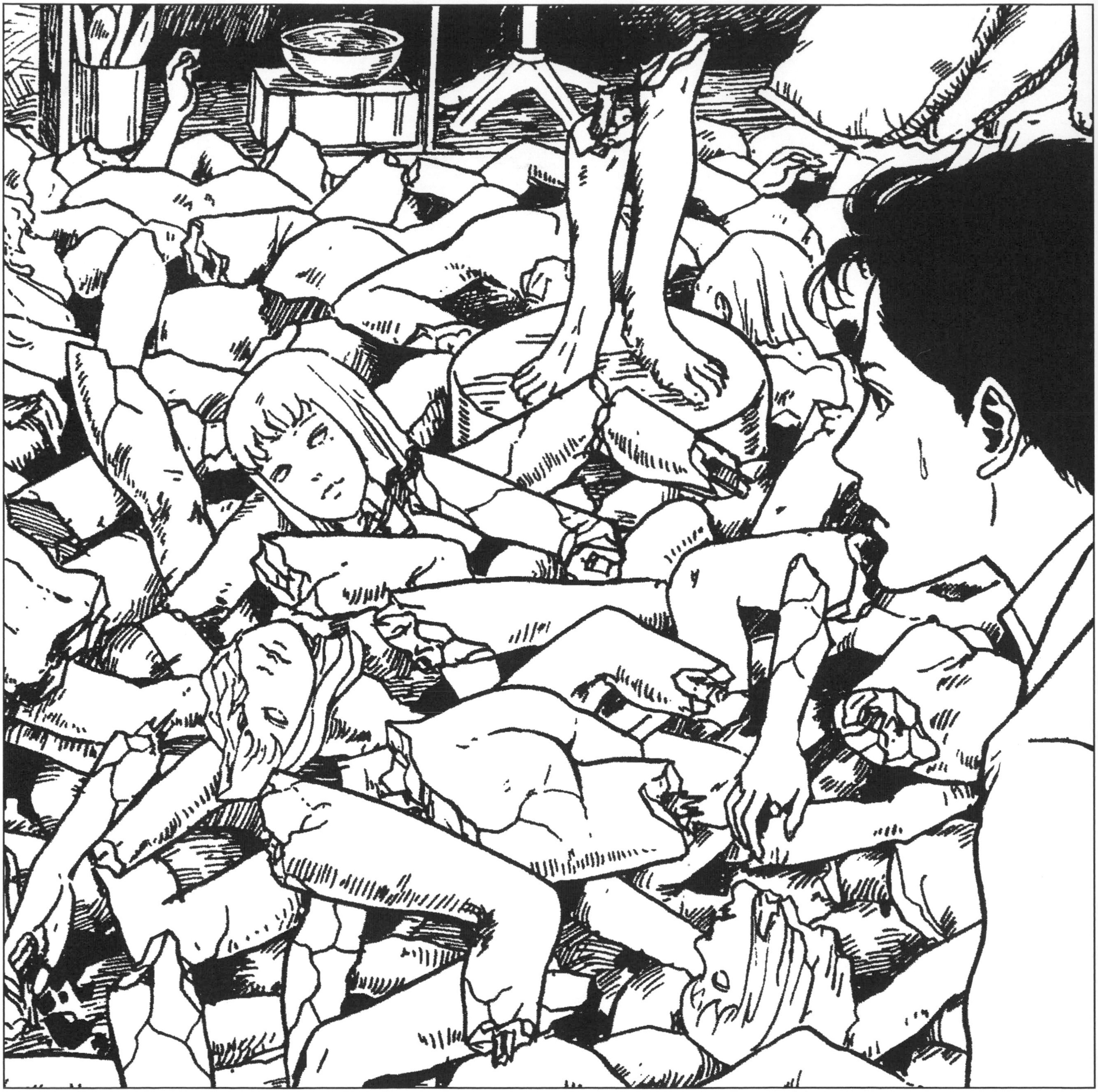

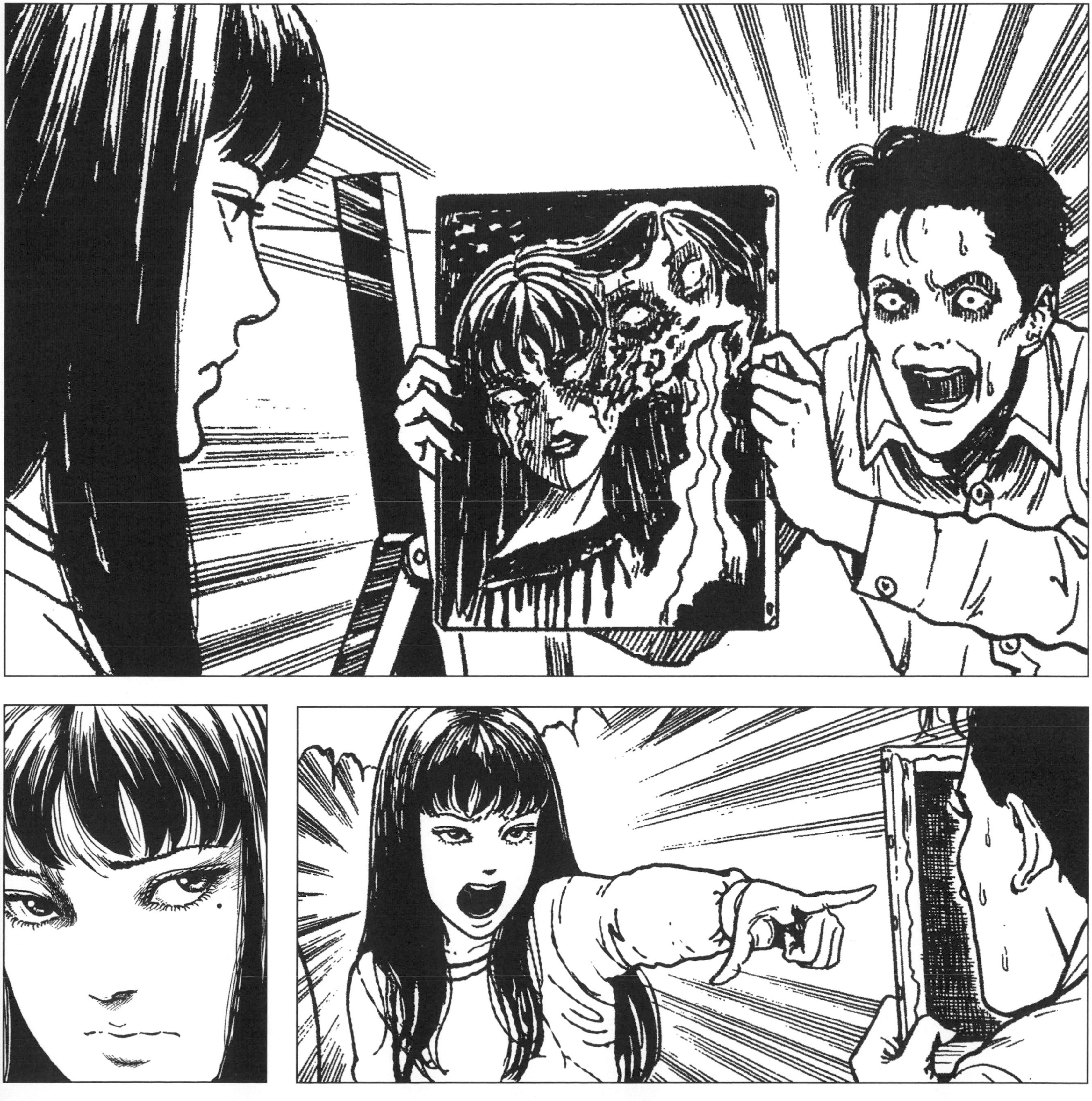

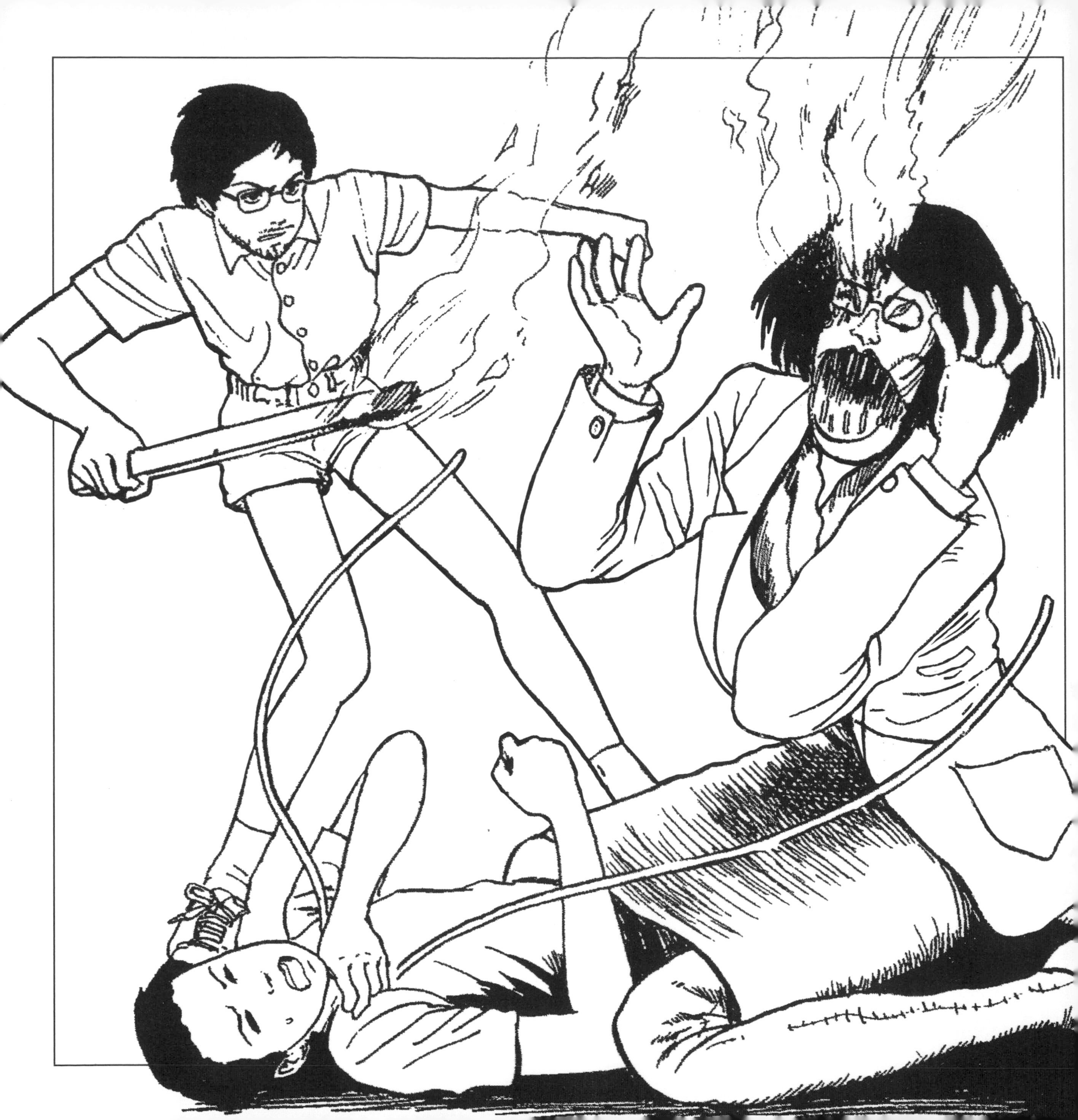

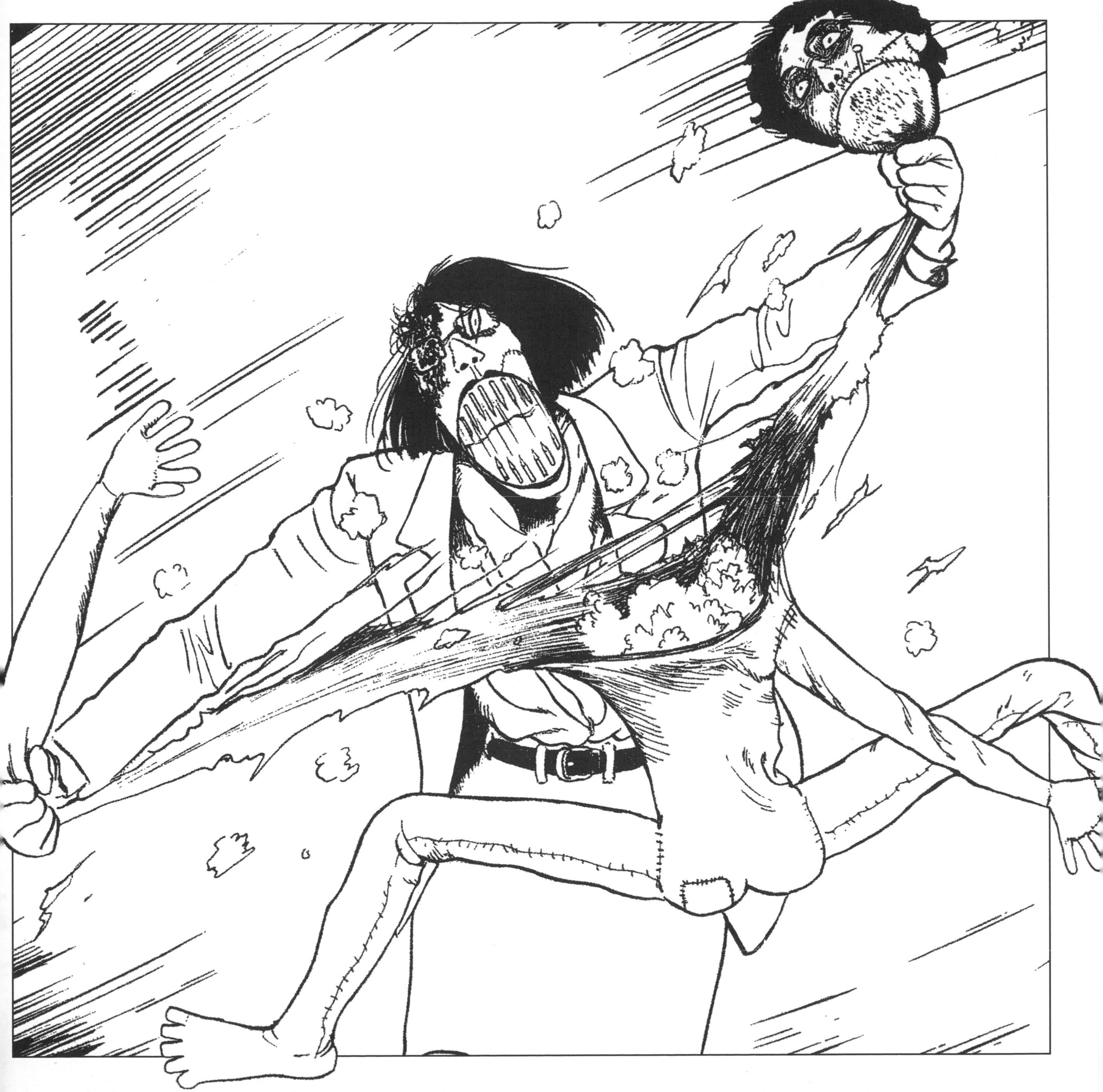

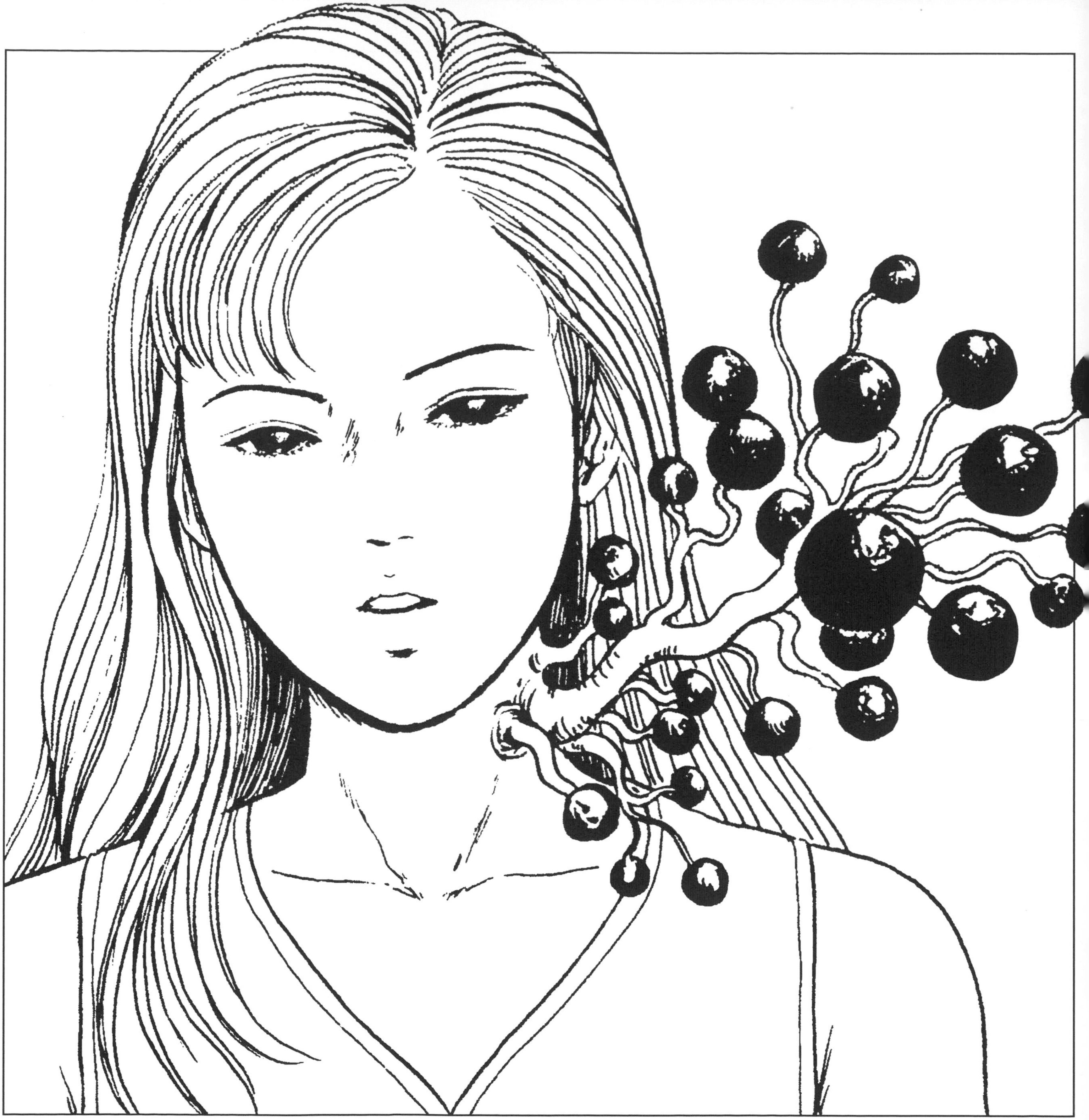

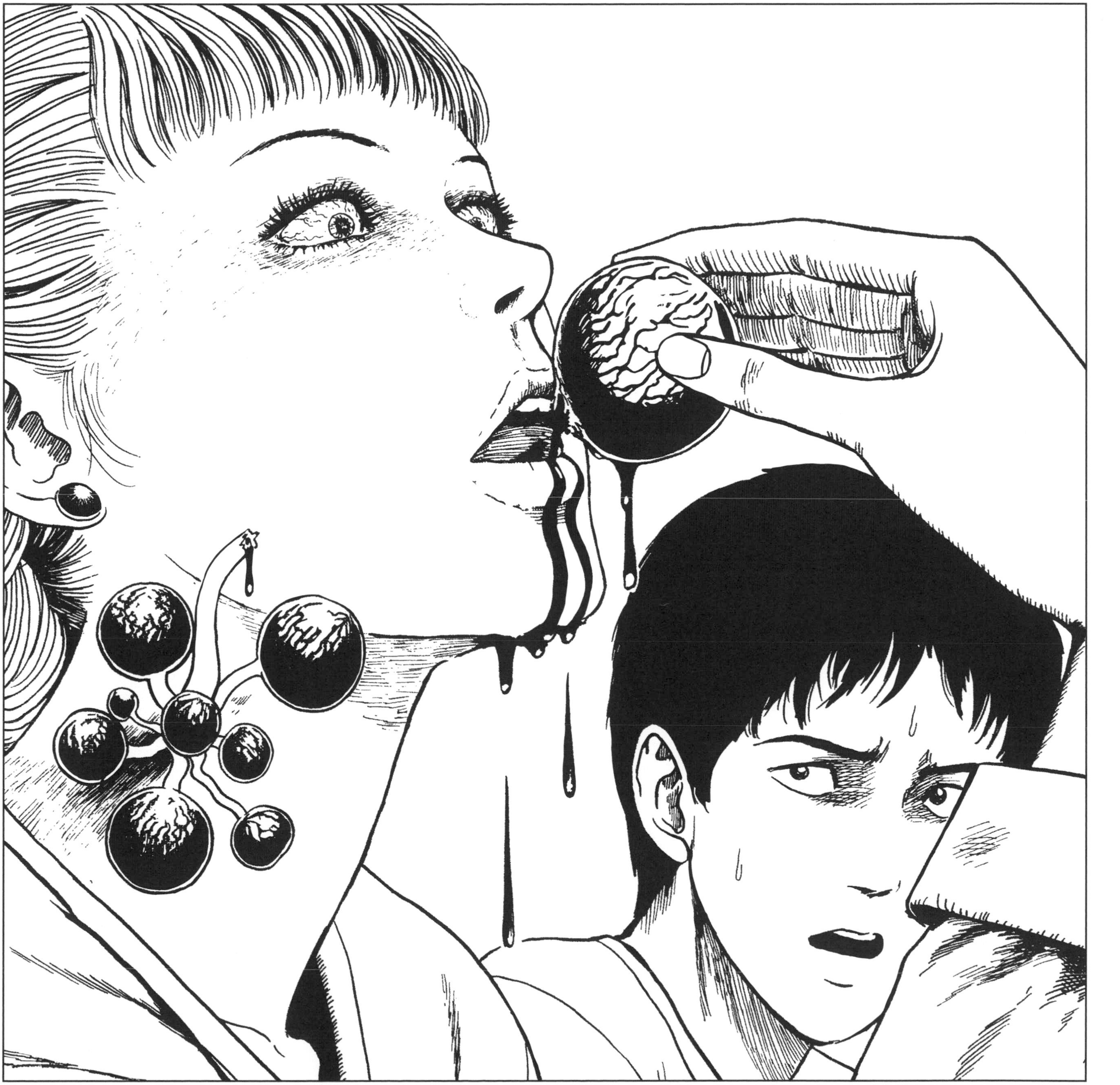

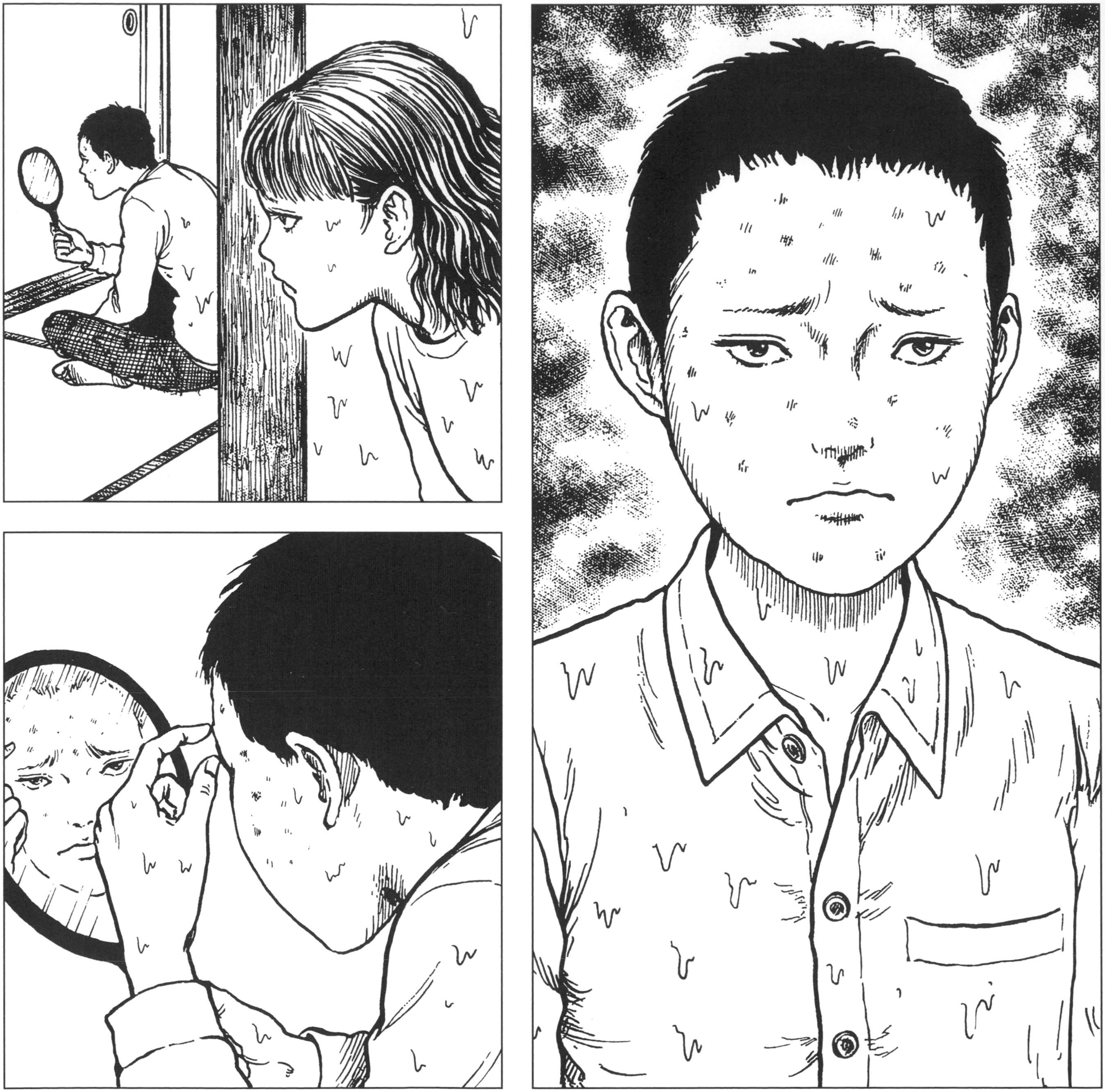

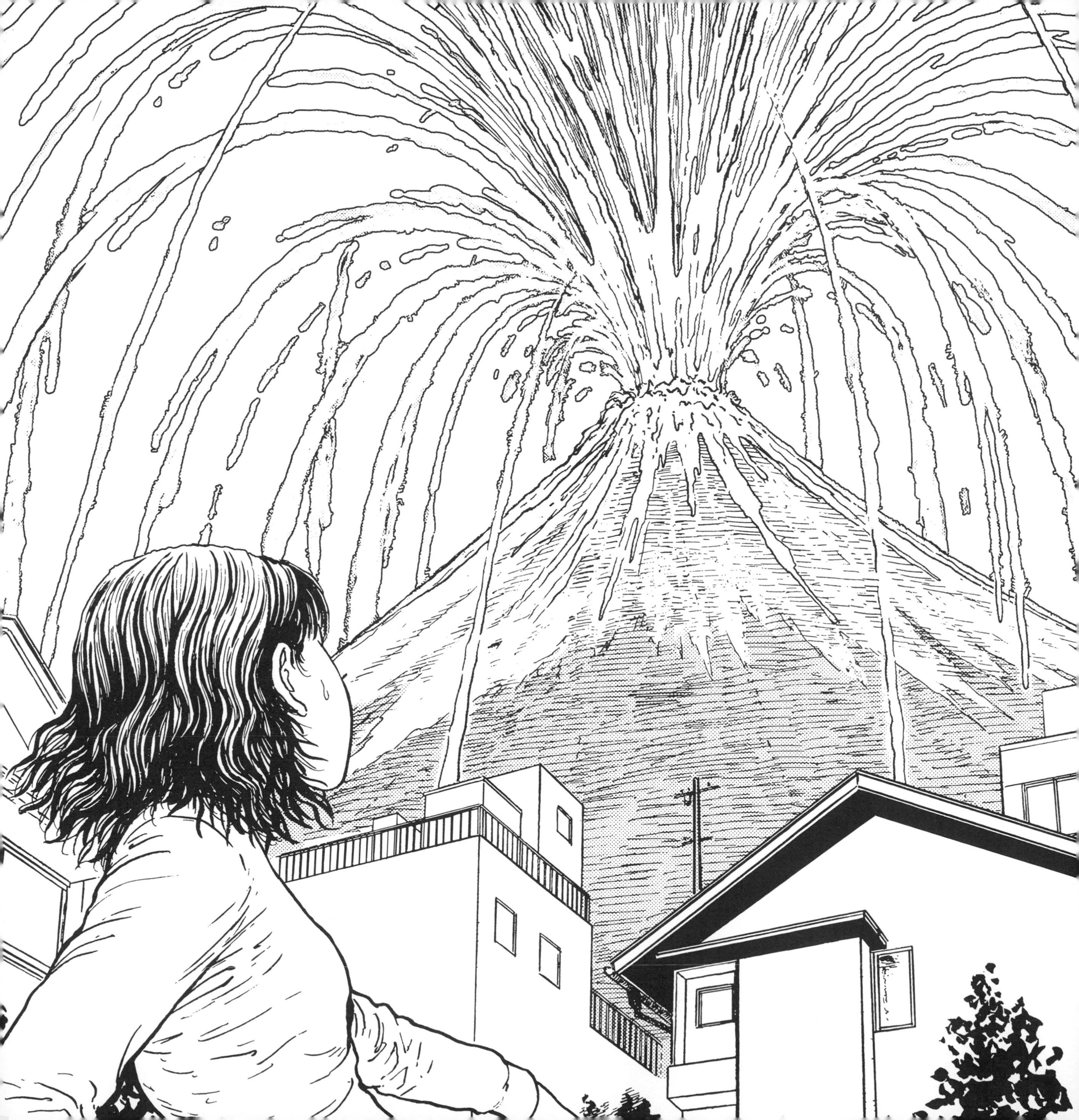

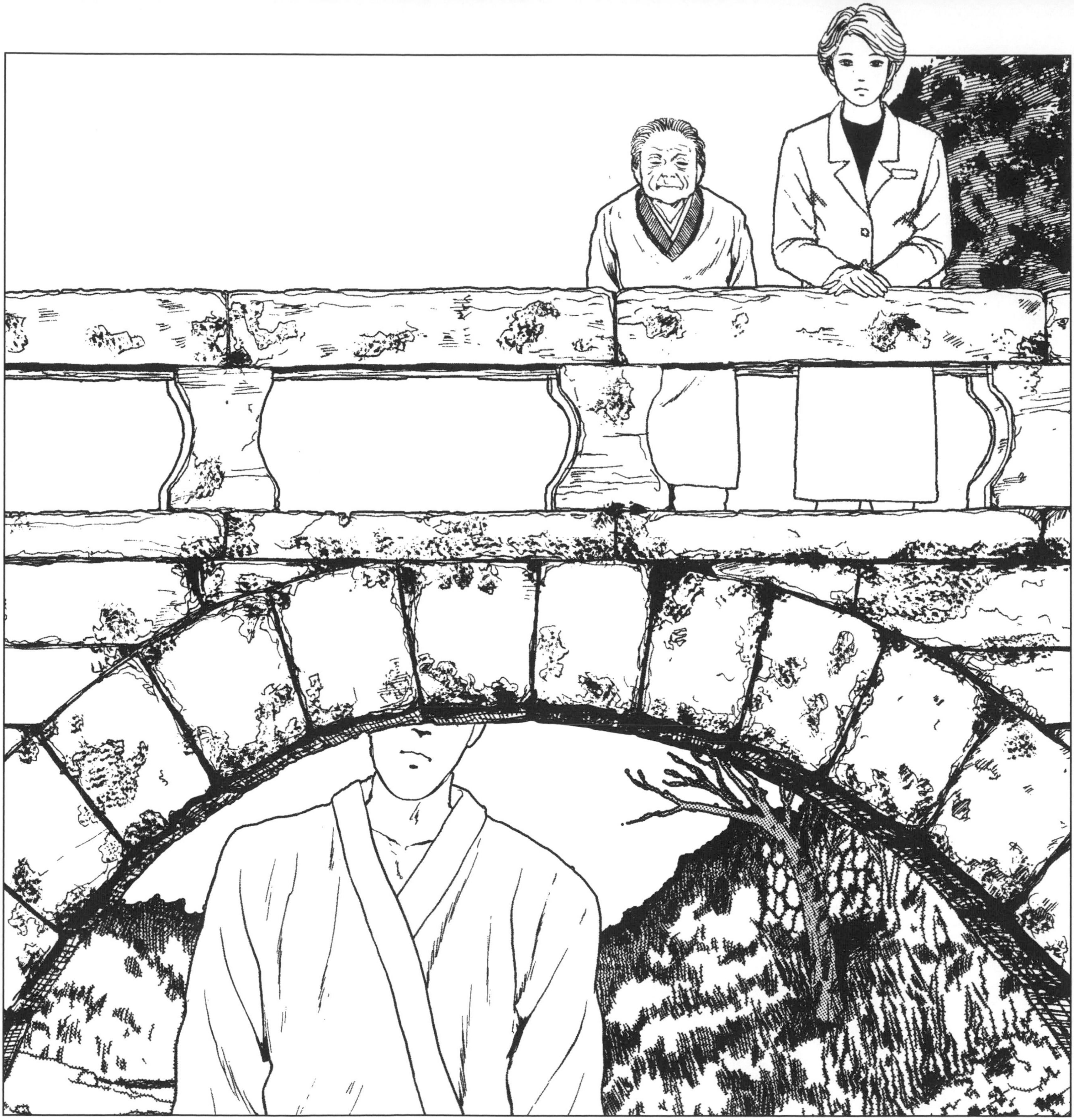

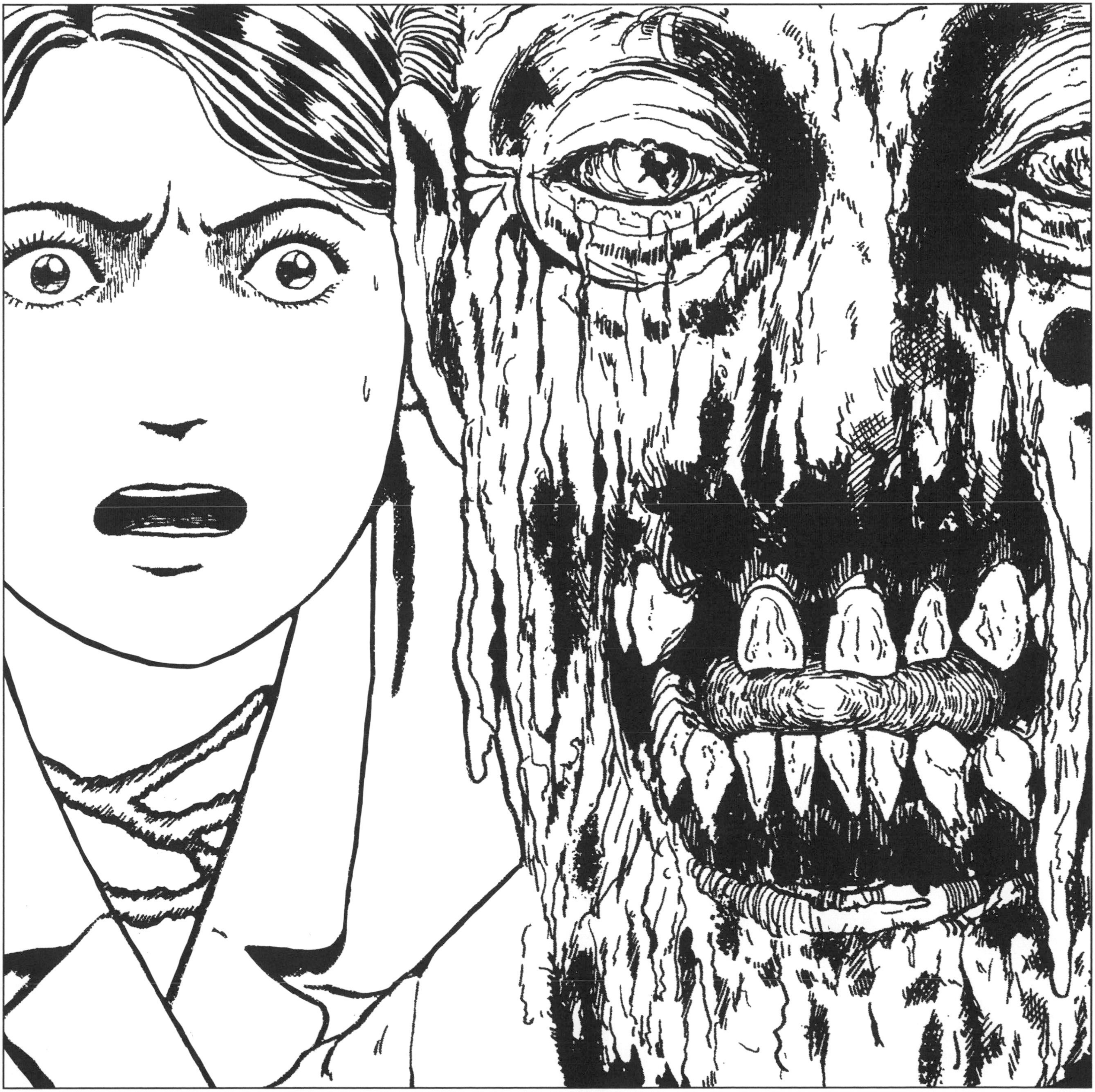

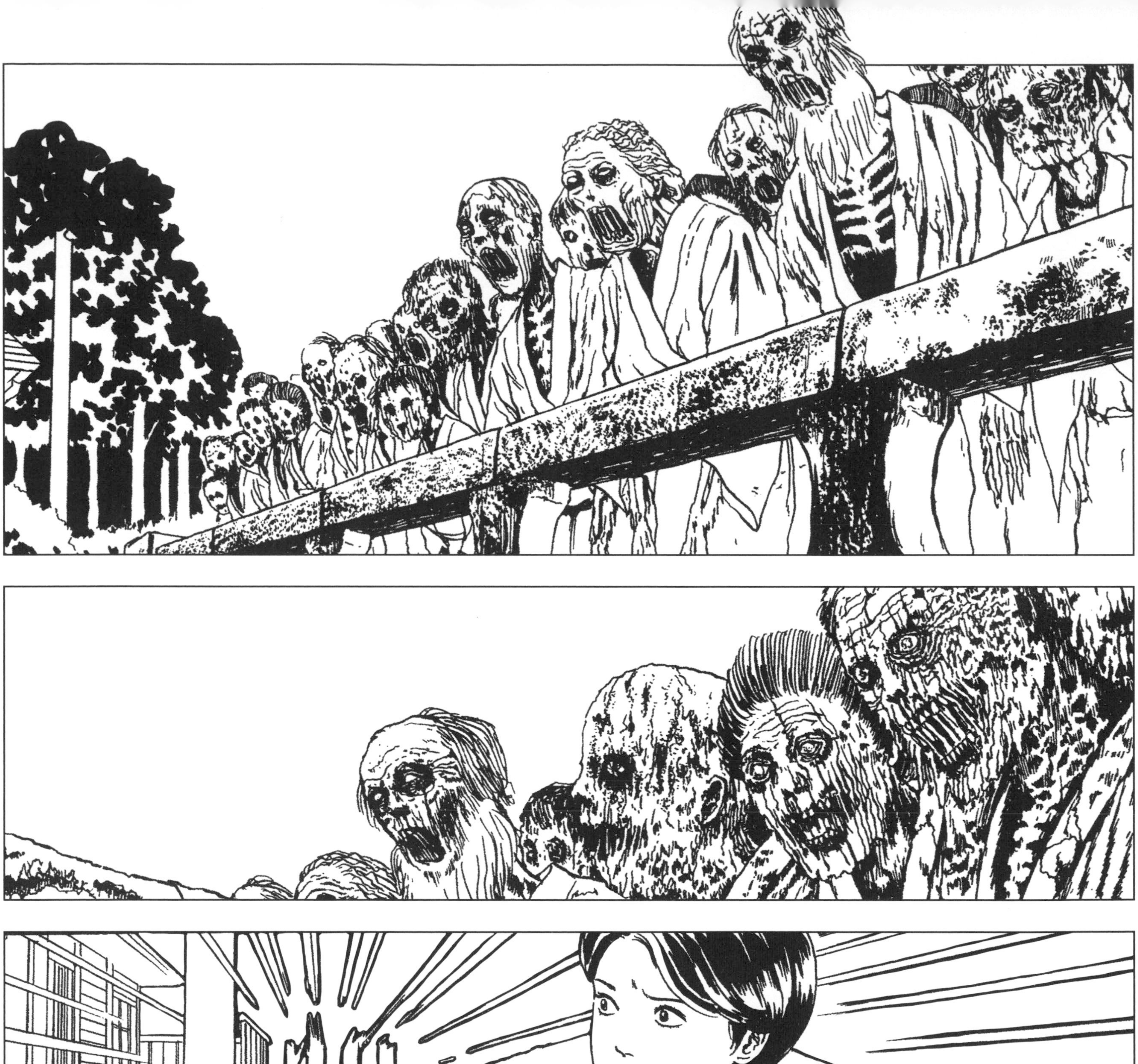

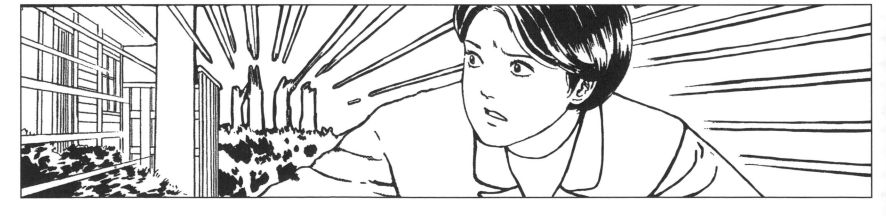

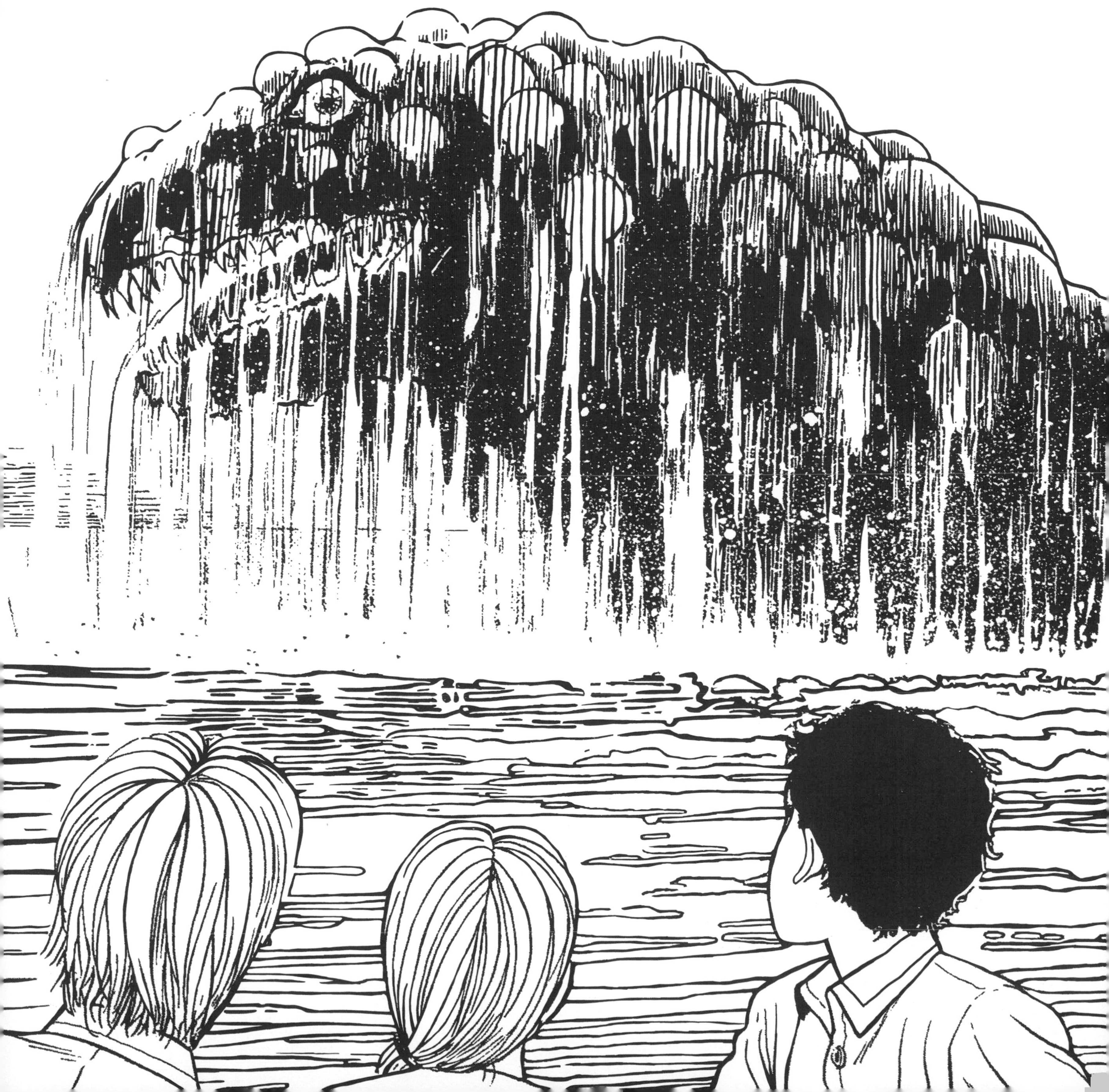

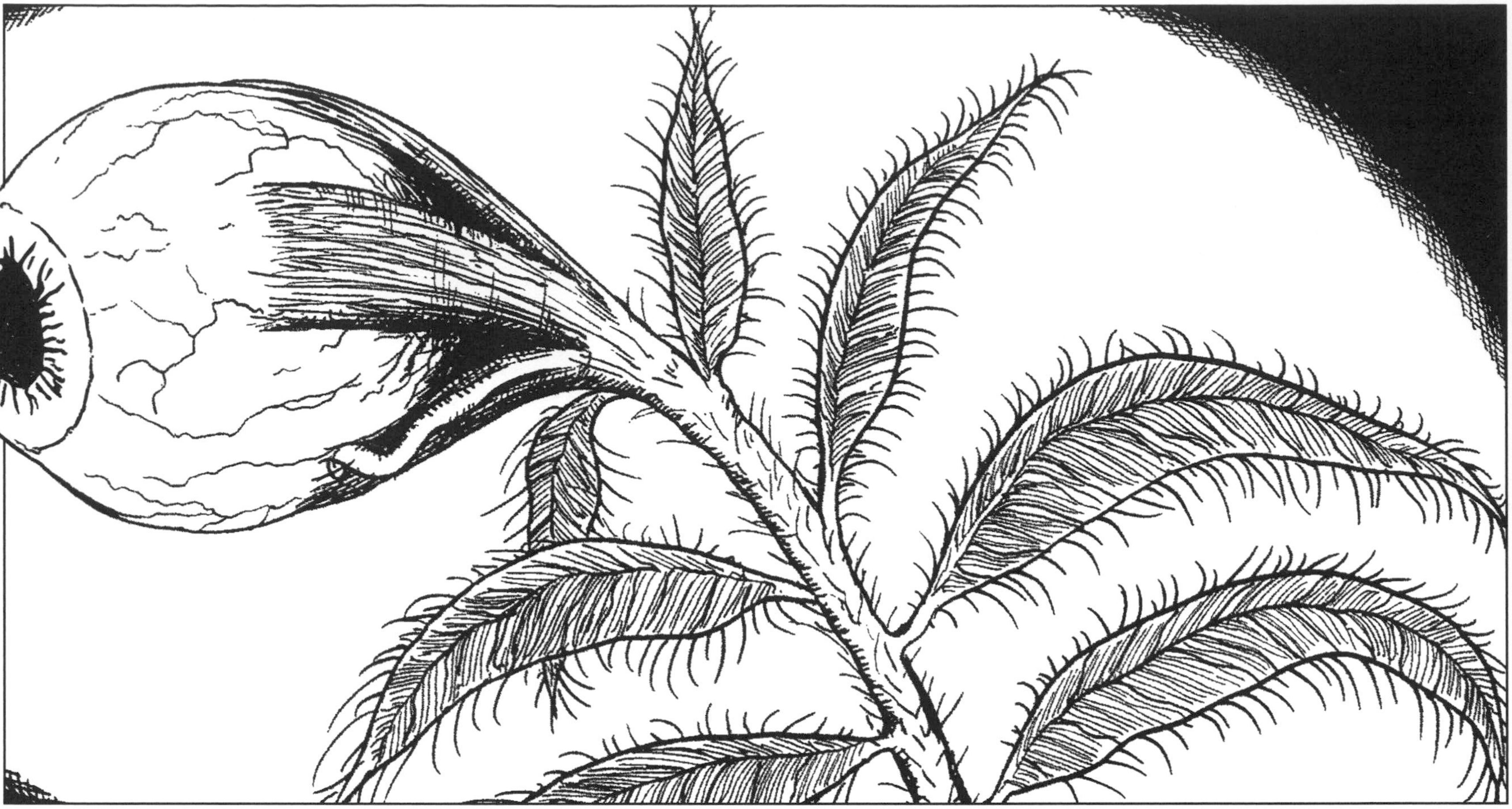
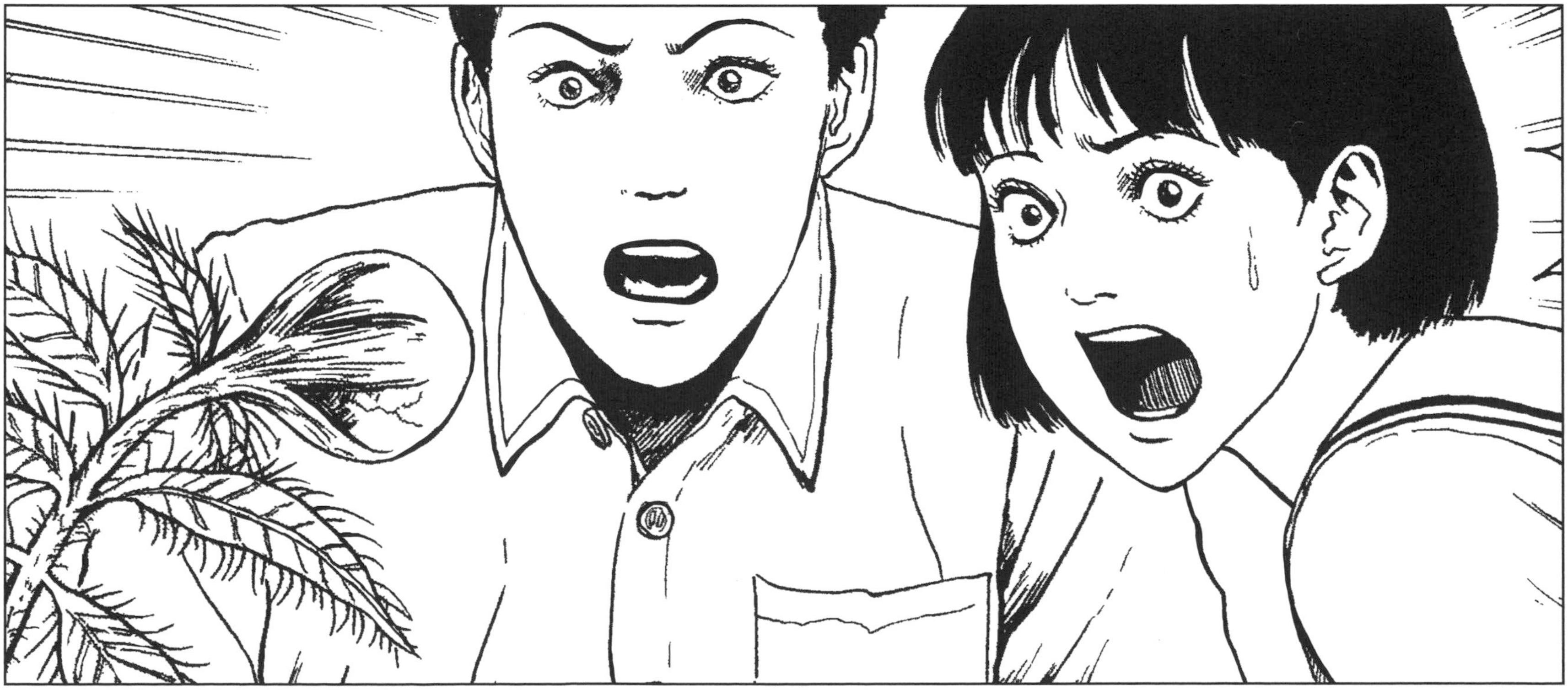

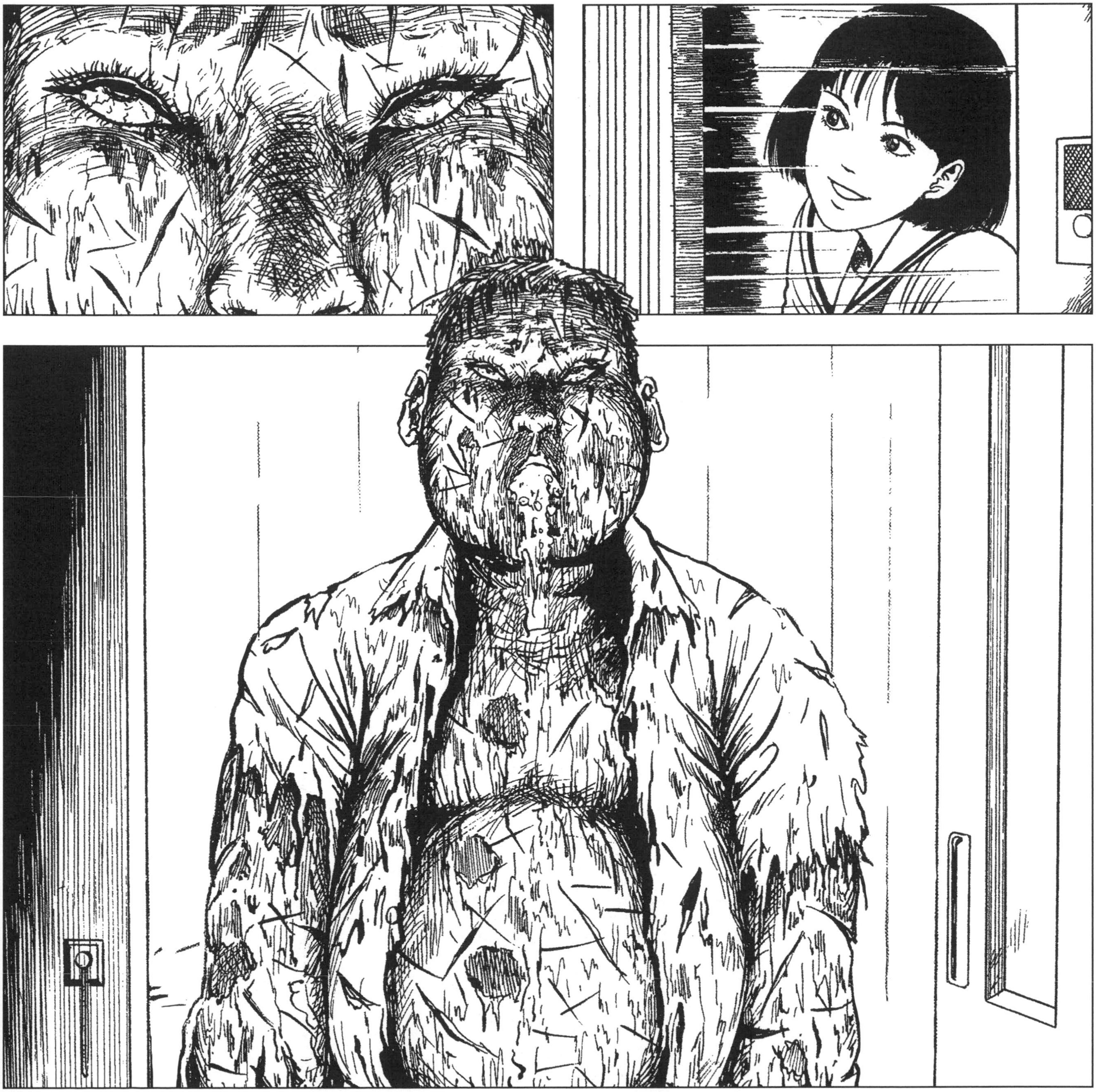

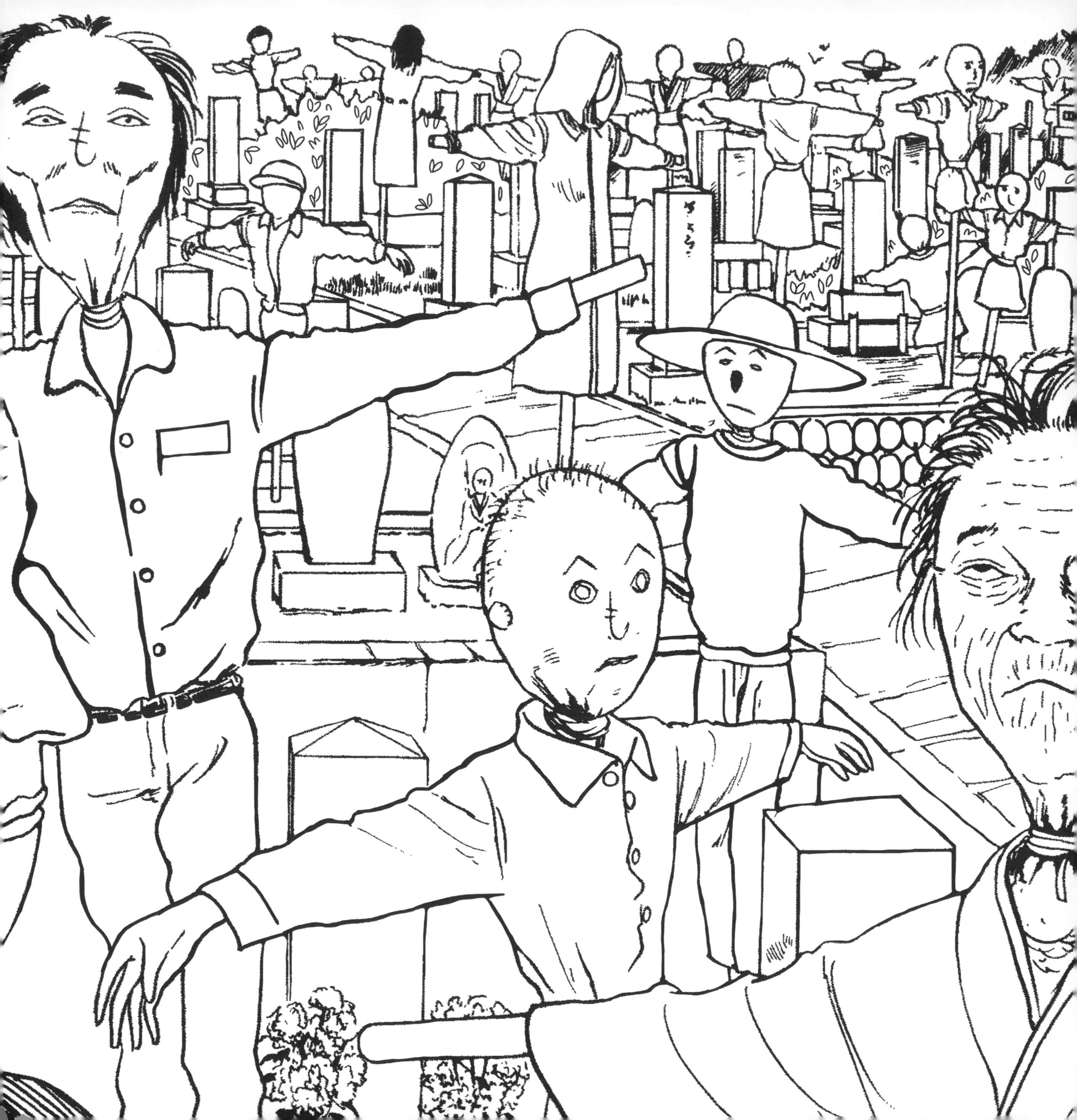

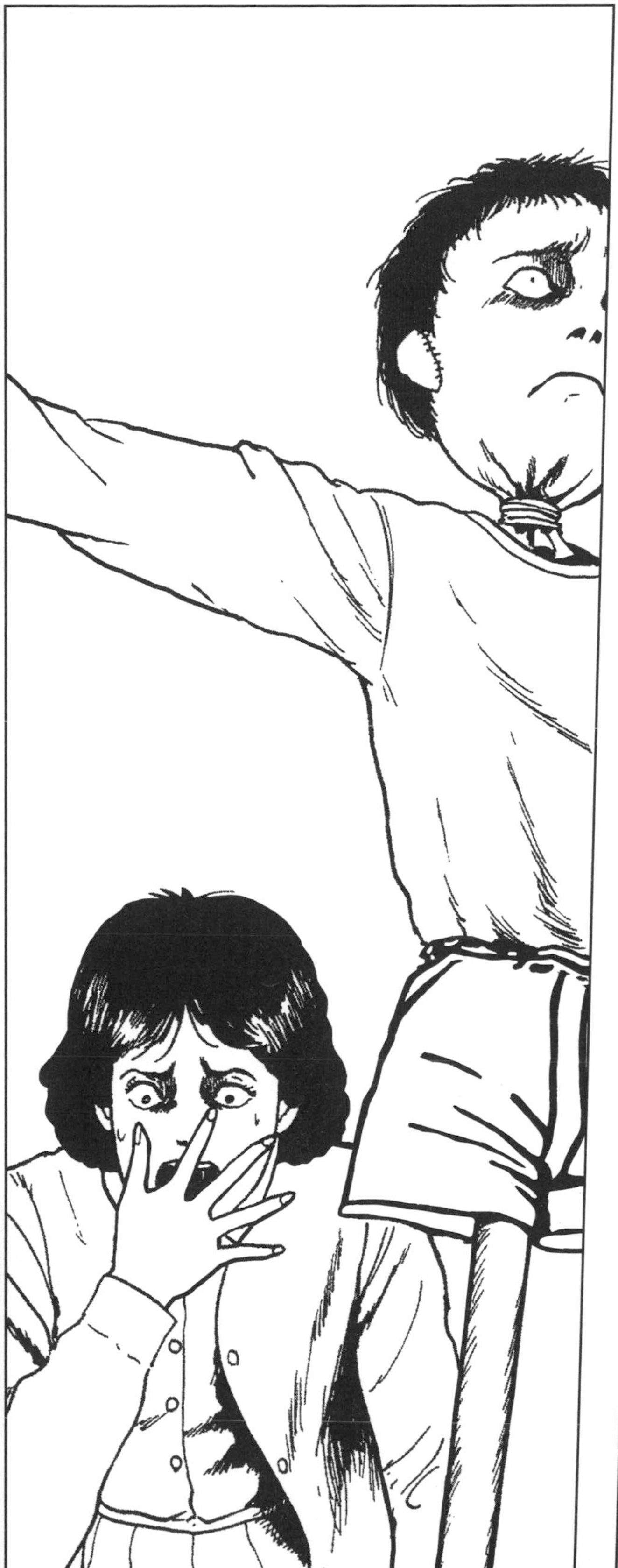

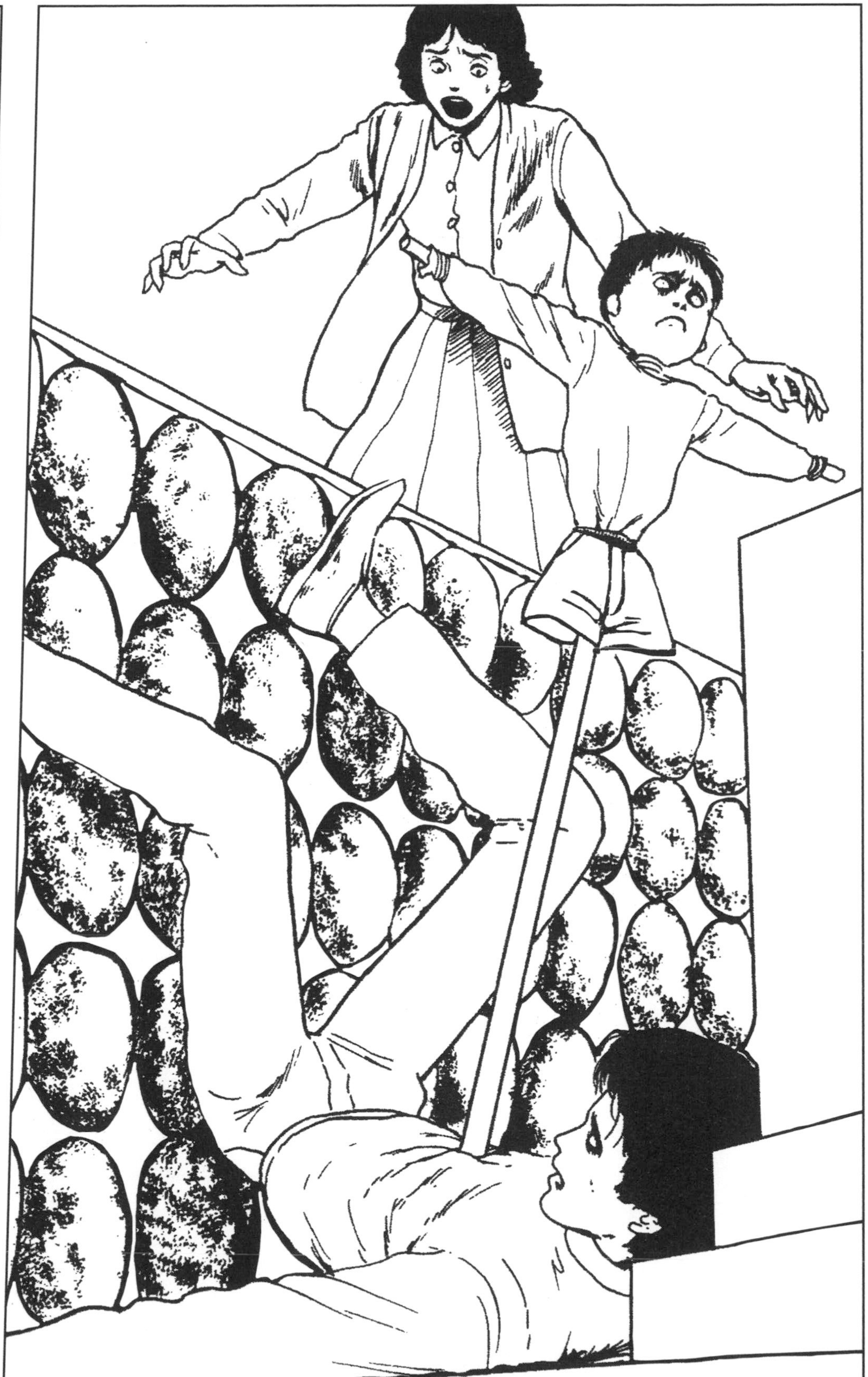

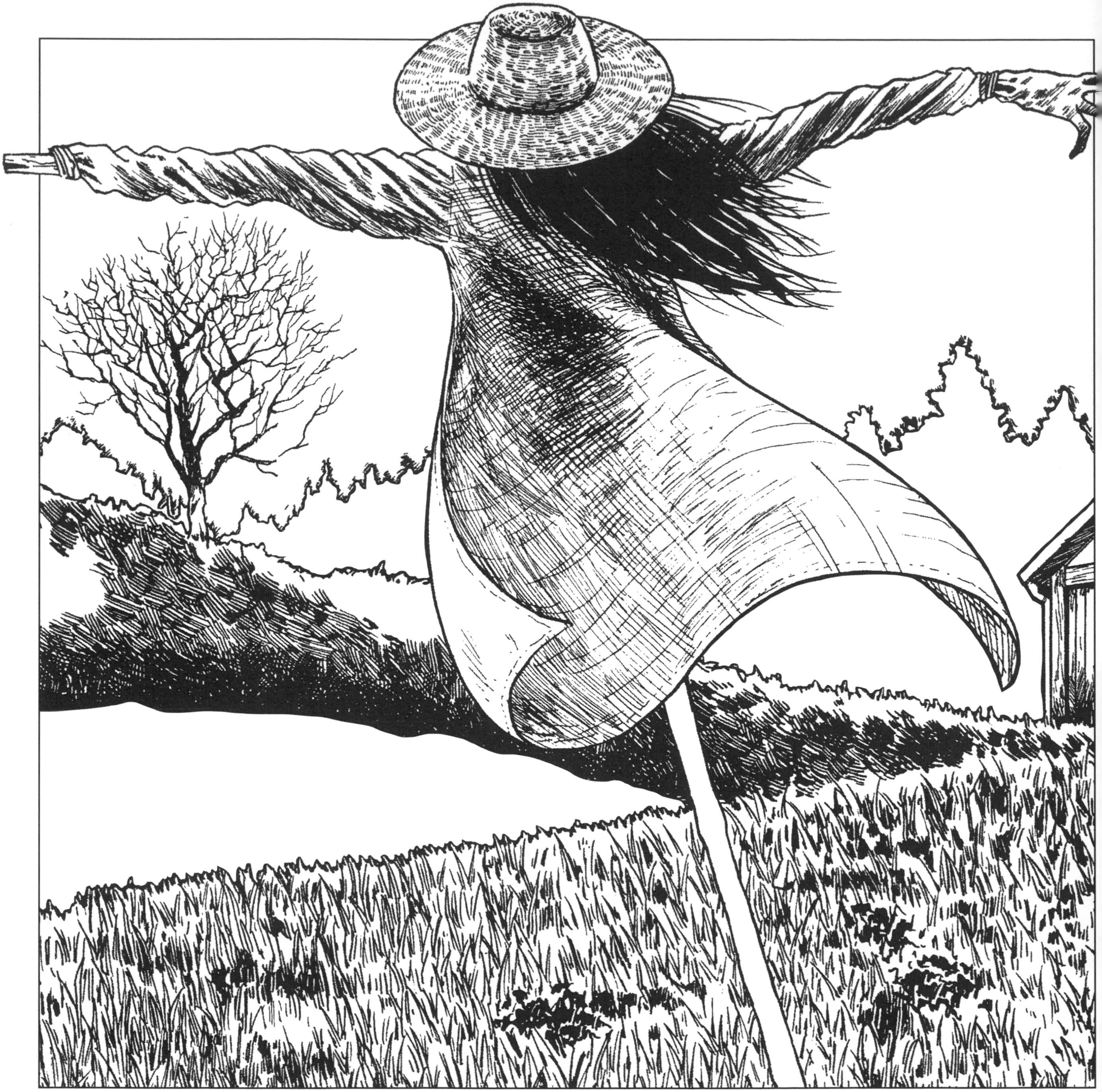

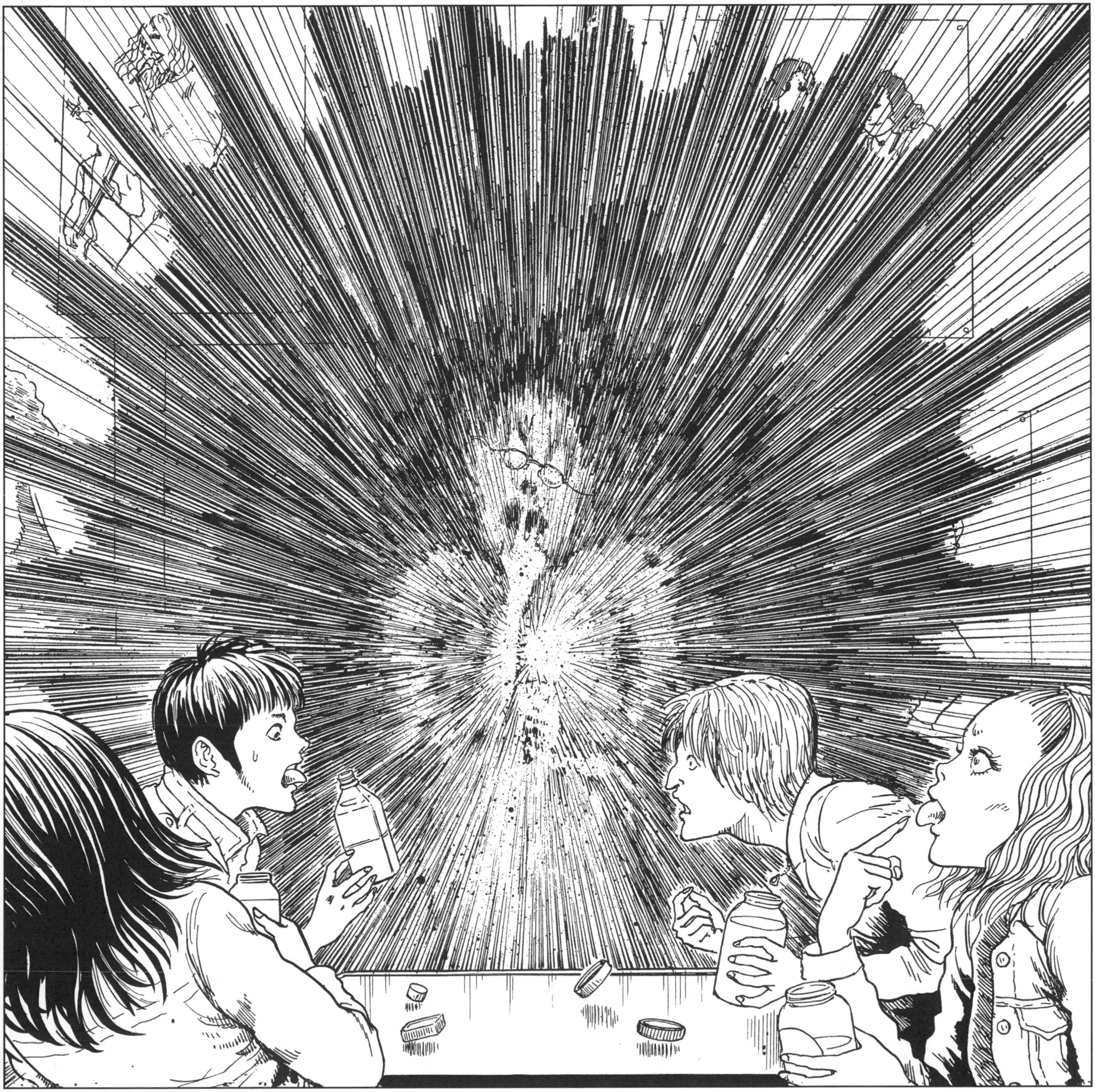

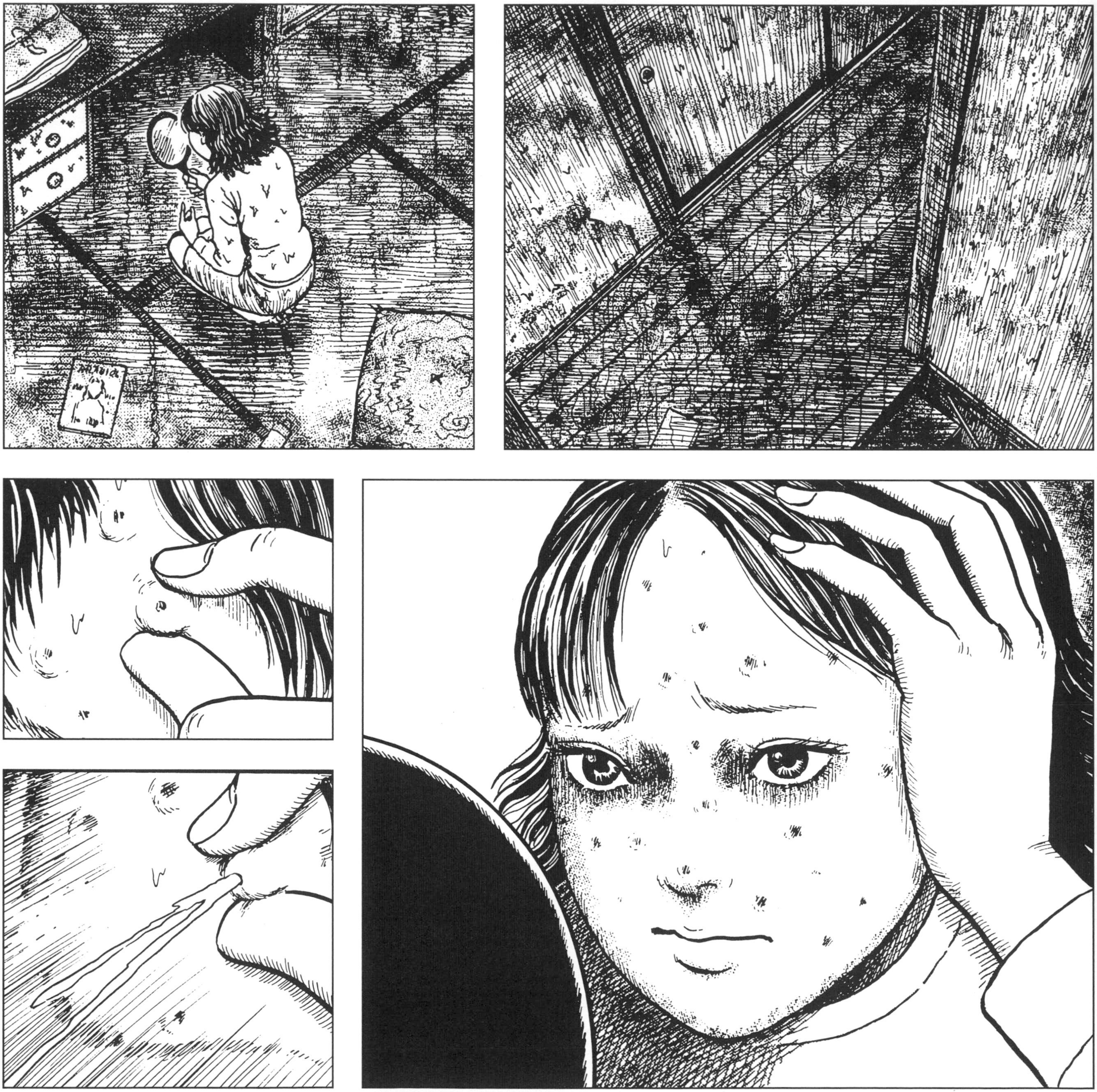

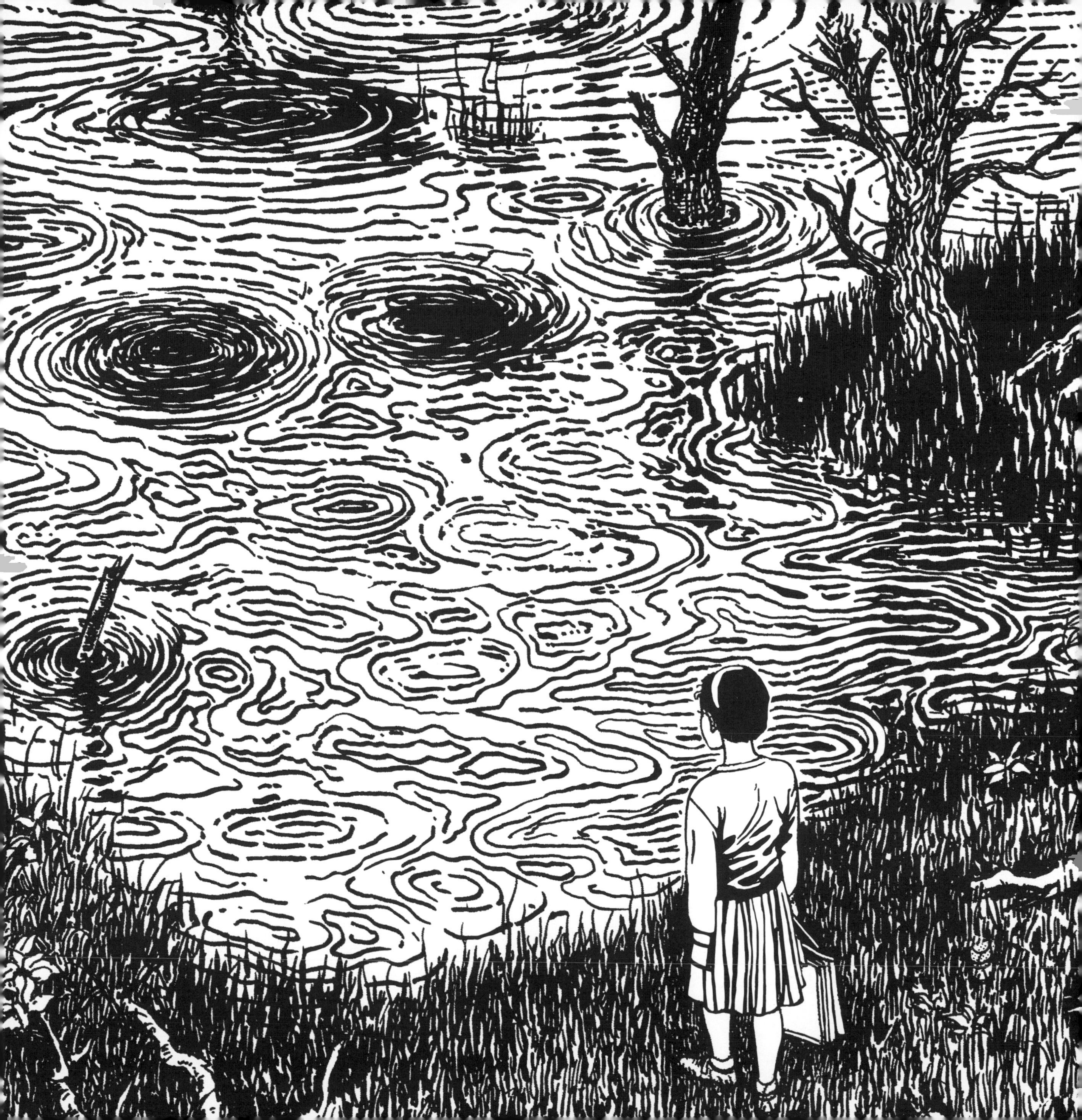

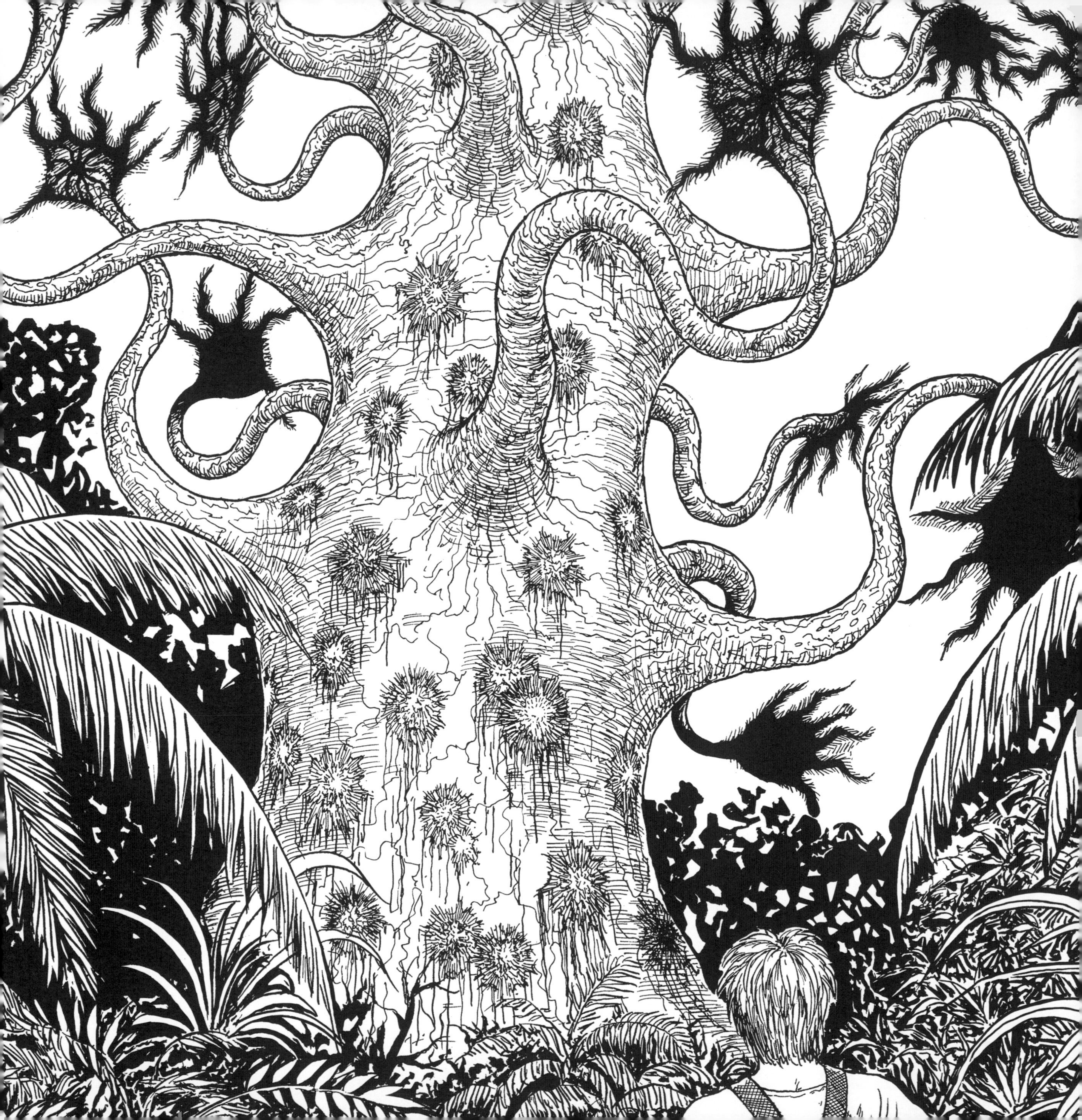

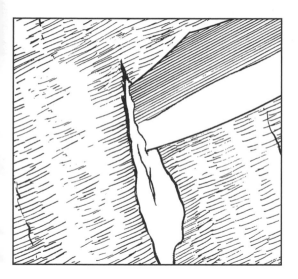

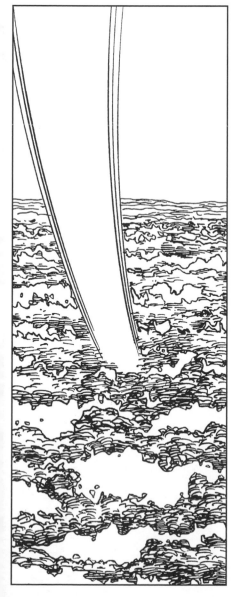

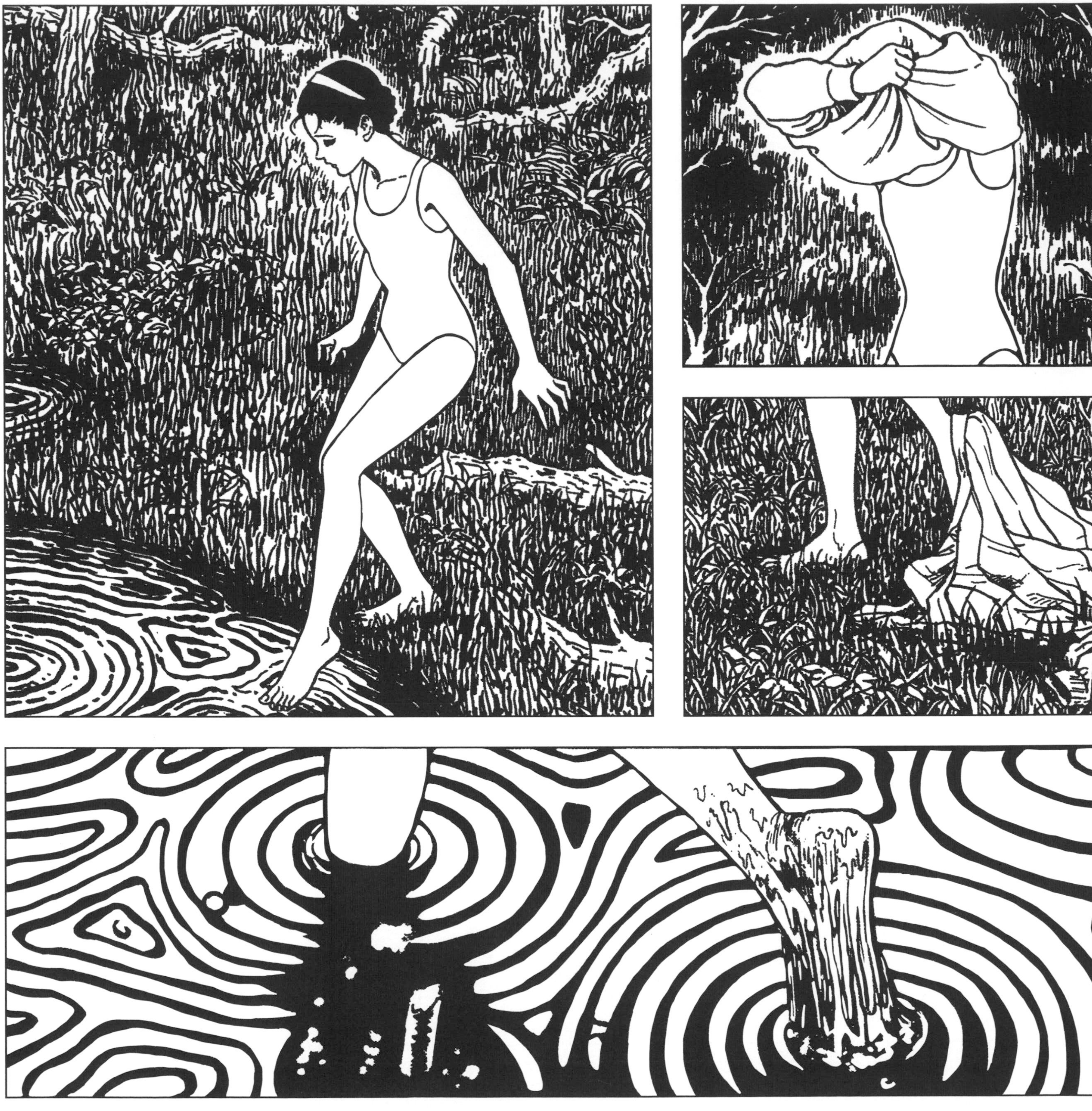

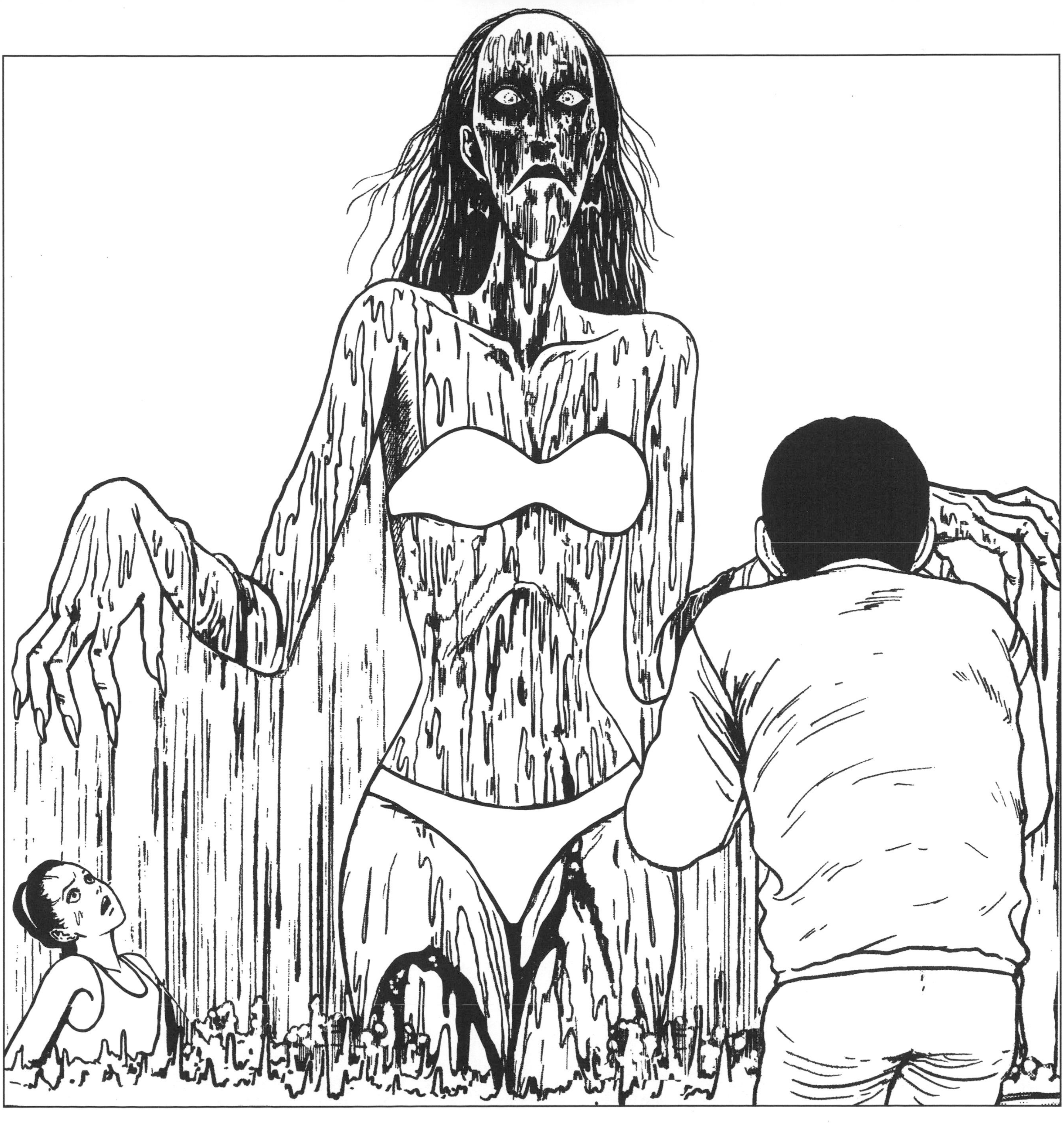

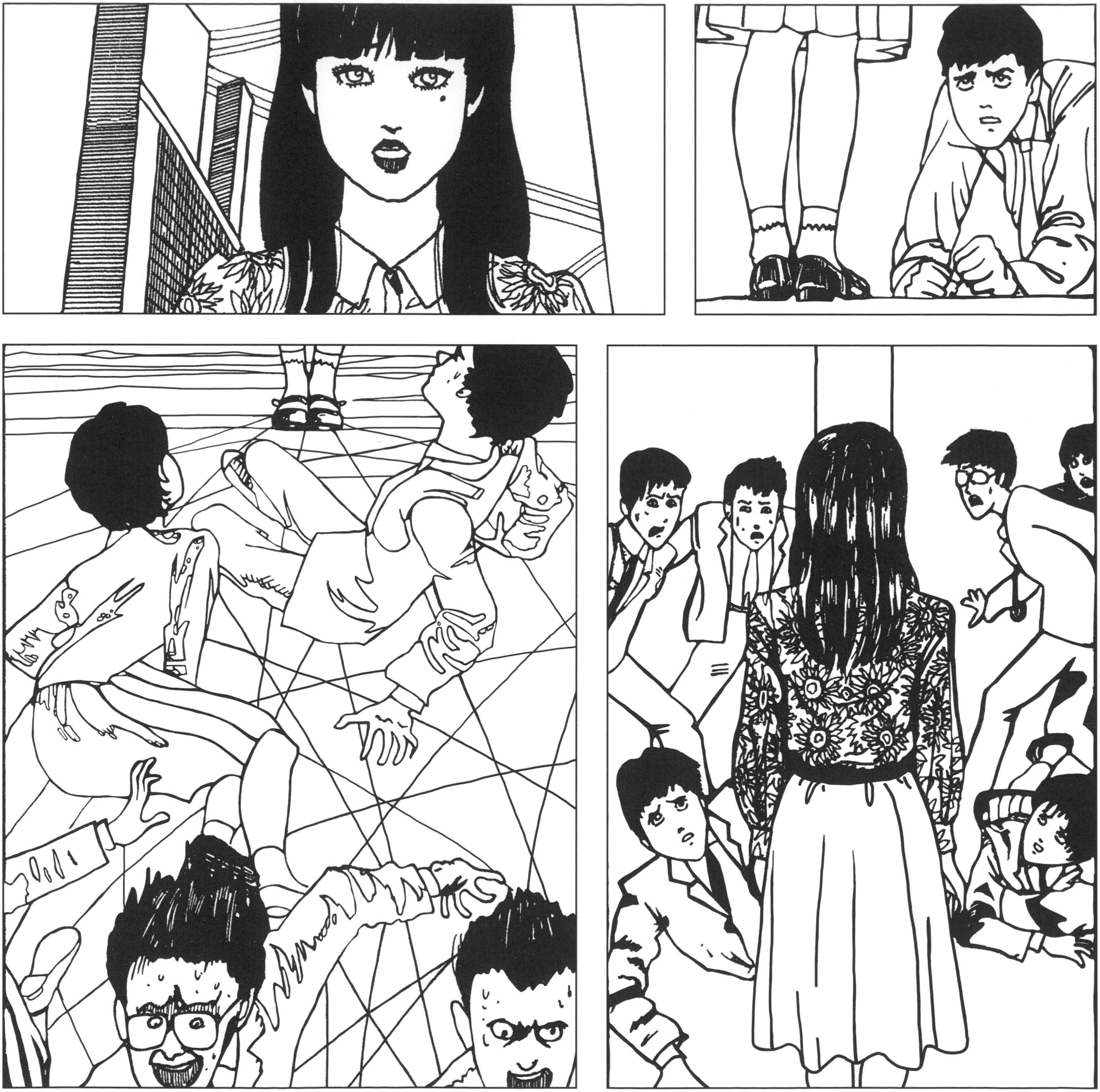

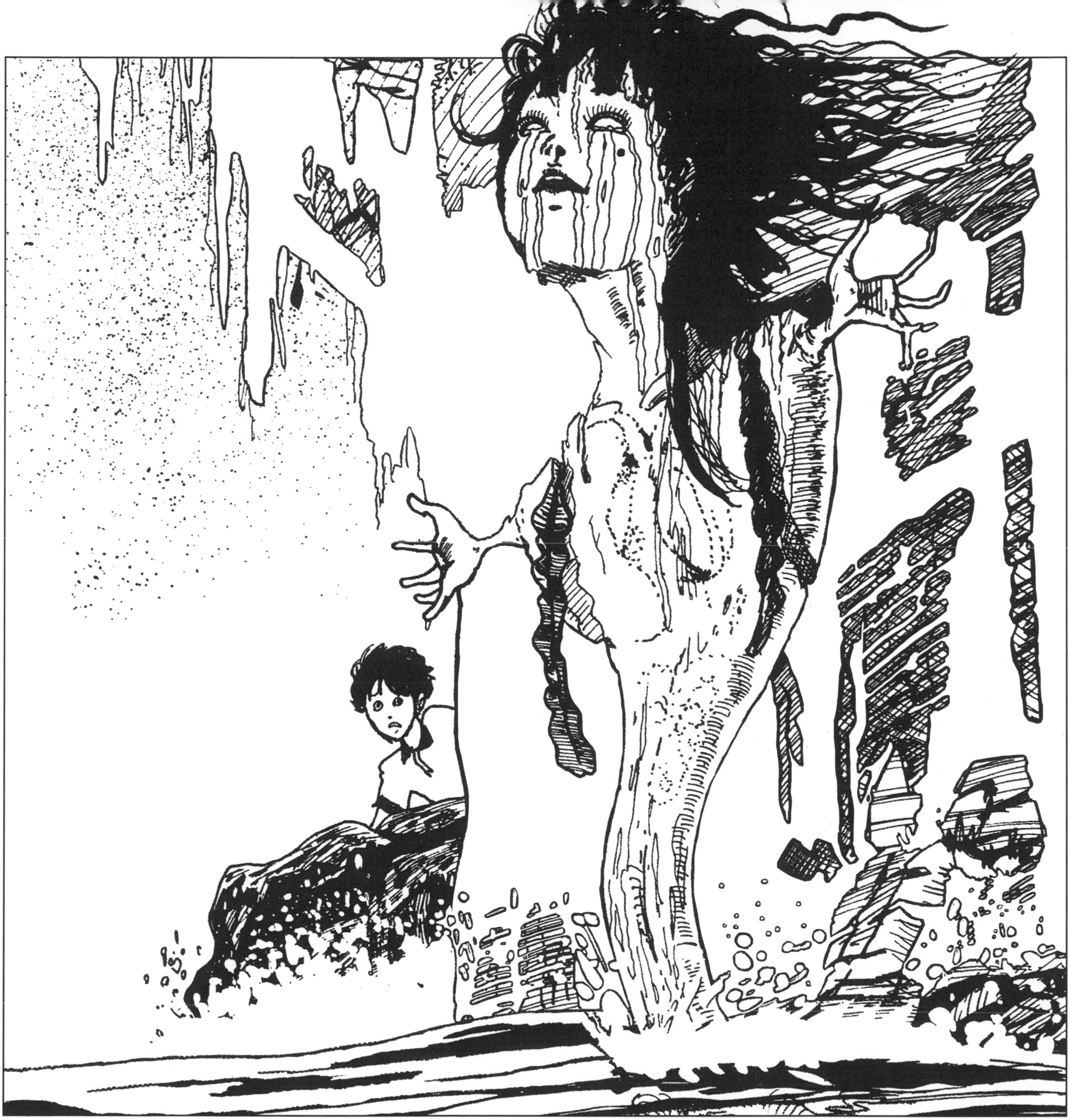

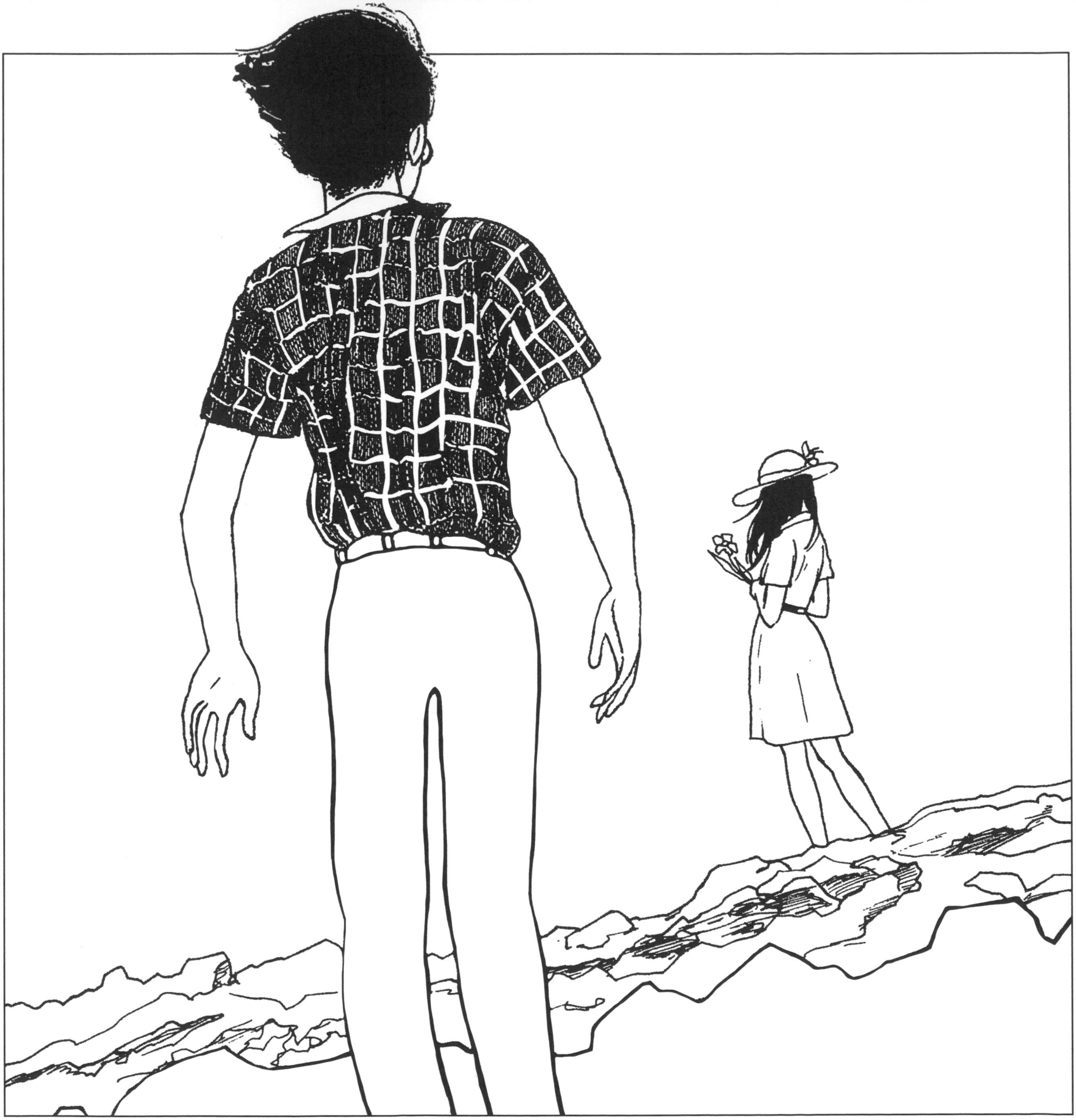

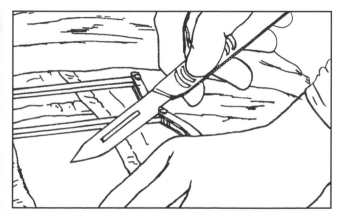
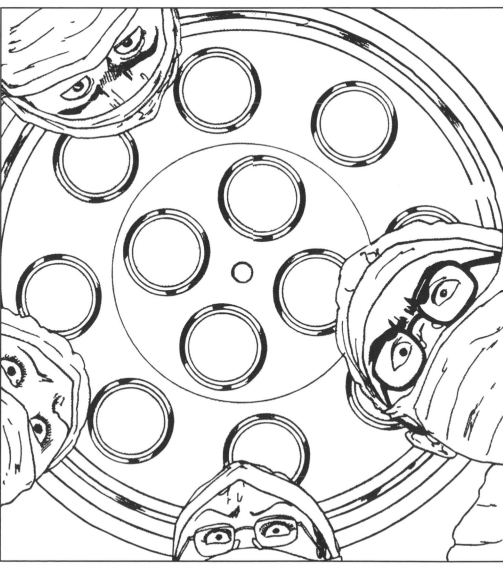

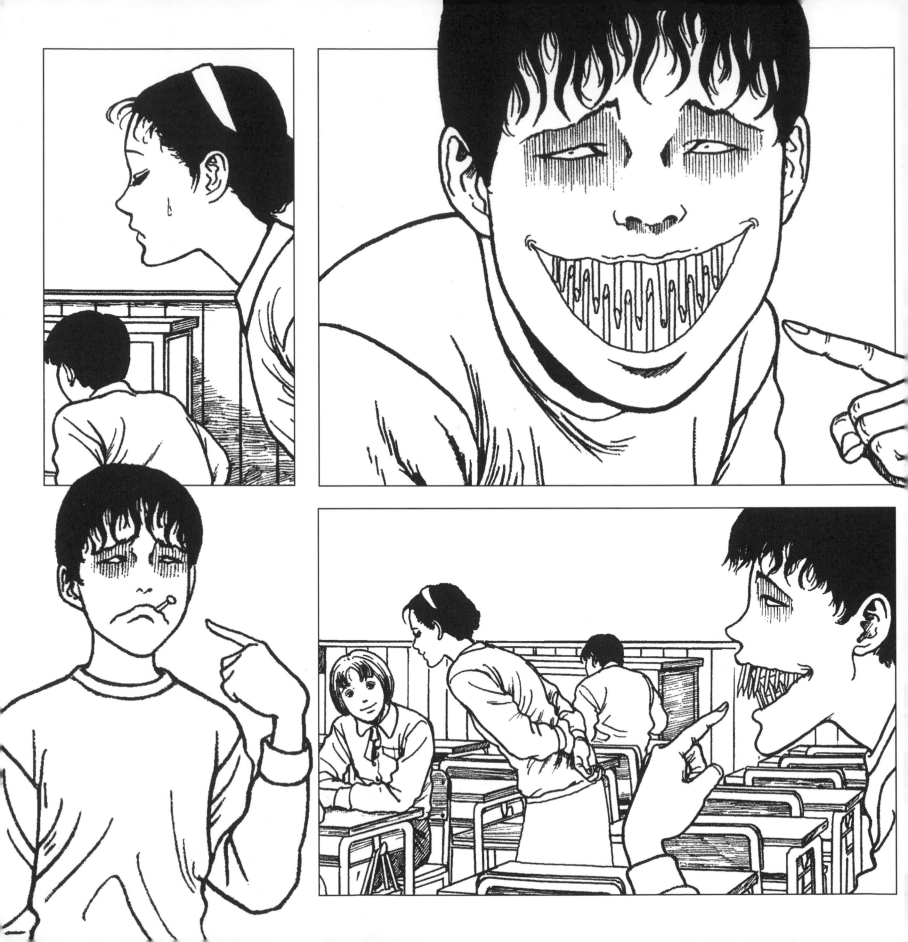